GAME ON

THE CHRISTIAN PARENTS' SPORTS SURVIVAL GUIDE

Jill Kemerer

Barb,
For all the times you've listened to me talk about this book — and for the million ways you've ministered to me — I'm so glad we're friends!

R · RIPPLE EFFECT PRESS

Jill Kemerer

Ripple Effect Press, LLC
Jill Kemerer
P.O. Box 2802
Whitehouse, OH 43571
www.jillkemerer.com

Scriptures taken from the Holy Bible, New International Version®, NIV®. Copyright © 1973, 1978, 1984, 2011 by Biblica, Inc.™ Used by permission of Zondervan. All rights reserved worldwide. www.zondervan.com The "NIV" and "New International Version" are trademarks registered in the United States Patent and Trademark Office by Biblica, Inc.™

Publisher's Note: This book is written as a source of information only. All efforts have been made to ensure the accuracy of the information contained in this book as of the date published. All scenarios in this book, with the exception of personal anecdotes involving the author's immediate family only, are fictional. Any resemblance to actual persons, living or dead, or actual events is purely coincidental.

Book Layout ©2017 BookDesignTemplates.com
Cover Design by James, GoOnWrite.com

Game On: The Christian Parents' Sports Survival Guide/ Jill Kemerer. -- 1st ed.
ISBN 978-0-9978179-0-4

Dedication

For my husband, Scott. Thank you for believing in this book and encouraging me to write it. Your faith in me means more than you'll ever know.

For our children, Olivia and Brandon. It's a privilege to watch you play.

For all the parents trying their best to keep youth sports in perspective. I salute you!

Contents

Introduction

I'm sitting on the bleachers at my son's baseball game. Every season I tell myself I'll stay calm. I won't let the sport consume my life. It's just a game, right? Yet, the season has barely begun and I feel myself losing it. Big time. I want to be a shining light—a positive role model—but I'm pretty sure I'm morphing into the princess of darkness.

As frustration builds inside me, I clutch my hands together. I don't want to be like this. Why do my kids' sports mean so much to me? I'm not even the one playing!

I keep it together until the game ends, but as I drive home my spirits sink. It doesn't matter what sports my kids are playing, I get emotionally invested, too invested. It's a vicious cycle that begins during preseason practices and ends shortly after the final game. I can't seem to break free from its grip, and I'm tired of deluding myself that I can.

Later that night, I do a quick online search for books written for parents with children in sports. I find plenty of nonfiction *about* kids' sports, especially ones teaching technique, and there are a few guides to help children deal with sports. However, there aren't many books written expressly for parents. I want a book to help *me* through the highs and lows of youth sports.

The information I crave doesn't seem to be there. Then it hits me. I'm a writer. In addition to my published novels, I've written over one thousand nonfiction blog posts.

I will write the book I'm searching for.

The moment feels triumphant, tremendous. Until fear crashes down. How can I write a book to help parents when I'm clueless? I'm not a psychologist or an expert about sports. I'm just a stressed-out mom trying to do her best and coming up short.

But, if I write it, maybe it will help someone like me.

I've sat through basketball games, gymnastics practices, tennis lessons, volleyball tournaments, football scrimmages, baseball games, track meets, swim lessons, cross country races, softball games, dance recitals, and soccer games. I've driven to countless practices, loaded my van with gear and bottled water, and spent weekends in distant cities for tournaments.

While I've loved (and continue to love) every minute of supporting my kids, I haven't always loved what it's done to me. This is a survival guide for Christian parents who are uncomfortable with the politics and pressures of youth sports. I'm sharing the emotional challenges I've faced as well as the methods I've used to keep sports in perspective and to be the role model my kids need me to be.

Here's the thing, though, I've never done it alone. I *can't* do it alone. My faith in the Lord sustains me. The Bible is full of God's promises, and they apply to us today. We have a God who loves us with an all-consuming passion. God cares. About you, about me, about our kids. And yes, He cares about every part of our lives, even sports. But what we want for our kids—to be the best, to win—isn't always what will help them grow into mature adults.

The very things we as parents will go to great lengths to prevent our kids from experiencing are the ones that build their confidence, sharpen their ambition, and turn them into strong, moral people. Simply put, our kids need to struggle to mature.

It's easy to encourage our children through the highs in sports, but it's not as easy to be a voice of reason through the lows. That's parenting, though. We're there for all of it—the good, the bad, and the average seasons.

I hope this book gives you clarity about what you want your child to get out of sports and the tools for you to handle the challenges with grace. I can't guarantee you'll be calm or stress-free at games, but at least you'll know you are not alone!

CHAPTER ONE

Why Are They Playing?

"Fix these words of mine in your hearts and minds; tie them as symbols on your hands and bind them on your foreheads. Teach them to your children, talking about them when you sit at home and when you walk along the road, when you lie down and when you get up." Deuteronomy 11:18-19 (NIV)

Your daughter made the team! You can't help but pump your fist into the air. She spent countless hours practicing, and it's all paying off. It wasn't a solo effort, though. You've toiled right there with her. You've sacrificed time to drive her to practices, money for the equipment and fees, and energy to help her any way you could. To think she beat out such a large number of kids—she's a superstar!

Well, maybe she isn't a superstar yet, but she's clearly good. You know the coaches will see her natural talent, and each season will be a little easier than the previous one. It's inevitable that she'll get better, move into a top position, and continue to advance to higher levels. Any doubts about her playing are quickly shushed. Sure, there will be a few intense parents and tough games, but your daughter stands out. Why worry about things that aren't likely to affect her? To celebrate, you take her out for ice cream.

We live in a sports-crazy world. Sports simultaneously unify us even as they're dividing us. Go to any college football rivalry game and you'll see what I mean. We high-five other fans and smack-talk our opponents. We anticipate tuning in to games on television, and we spend big bucks to watch professional sports in person. Our hard-earned money goes to licensed apparel to support our favorite teams. For many of us, sports are a fun part of life.

They're also big business. Professional athletes are paid millions of dollars, wooed to sell products on television, written about in magazines, and interviewed on late-night talk shows. College athletes are discussed at a national level. High school athletes are celebrated locally with pride. Even younger athletes get a boost of respect from their peers.

As parents we want to give our kids every advantage we can afford. We help them with homework, advise them, feed them, clothe them, and teach them our values. It's only natural for us to encourage them to pursue a sport, too.

But *why* do we want our kids to play sports? There isn't a one-size-fits-all answer. Just as each family has its own moral code and set of priorities, each family also has its own reasons for signing kids up for sports.

Do you know why *you* want your kids in sports?

Everyone Else Is Playing

I never put much thought into why we signed up our kids to play sports until they were in middle school and the stress was getting to me. Maybe I thought I knew—I'd told myself vague reasons about them playing with their friends and being part of a team—but when I started researching this book I finally came face to face with my agenda.

It left me perplexed.

You see, I thought I had good intentions. Signing them up for gymnastics or tee-ball seemed as natural as enrolling them in pre-school or getting their annual health checkups. But as time wore on, the stakes grew higher, and one day I got real with myself. I realized my good intentions too often were overridden by pride.

It's normal to be proud of our children and to applaud the results of their hard work, but we have to be careful because pride can breed un-healthy competitiveness and insecurity.

Pride, unhealthy competitiveness, and inse-curity.

The trifecta of parent problems.

When I sat down and analyzed why our kids were playing sports, I was shocked. To be frank, it didn't take long for me to realize I'd gotten swept into all of the above. I'd been putting too much emphasis on immediate circumstances and hadn't been considering the long-term ef-fects on our children. To make matters worse, our family values were being directly chal-lenged by the culture surrounding us. I wanted our kids to become mature adults with morals, yet I was inwardly balking at what this entailed where sports were concerned. What I really wanted? Sports to be effortless for my children.

Basically, I wanted all of the good and none of the bad.

Too often parents face dilemmas where we end up compromising our values to ensure our children get what we want for them. We're motivated by love for our babies, but this motivation can cloud our judgment and lure us into poor behavior. The long-term consequences are detrimental to our kids.

Let's go back to when it all begins, to those early years when sports seem like fun and a way to get some exercise.

I'll sign Johnny up for tee-ball. His daddy loves throwing the ball to him in the backyard.

Susie sure is flexible. Maybe I should call the gymnastics center Kate's mom told me about.

Annie is bouncing off the walls. Hopefully, the local soccer club will burn off some of that energy.

We watch our babies practice in shirts hanging to their knees. We chuckle as they run in the wrong direction and are generally clueless about what to do. We sign up for the parent snack list and snap a few pictures.

Within a short period of time, we're surrounded by other parents who have kids playing on the team. We hear things like all-star tryouts, dance competitions, travel teams, swim clubs, and gymnastics levels. The pressure begins almost immediately. Sometimes our children are only five years old!

Being around other parents on the sport circuit can be terrific. I've been blessed to make good friends who cheer with me on the sidelines and bleachers. But it's also where the unhealthy competitiveness kicks in. Oh, so Tina is on the swim team? My Susie is just as good. Whether or not we can afford the extra classes or if our young daughter even wants to devote early mornings to becoming a world-class swimmer, we're signing her up.

Fast forward a few years when your eleven-year-old is playing on a travel softball team, your nine-year-old plays basketball on a tournament league, and your six-year-old is being asked to enroll in every dance class offered because the teacher thinks she's gifted enough to be on the competitive dance team next year. The eleven-year-old also plays tennis during the summer, and the nine-year-old wrestles in the winter. Suddenly, our lives have become very full.

We're caught up in an expensive, time-consuming, and accepted (hey, who doesn't have friends with kids in *more* activities than ours) cycle of youth sports.

As we try to figure out how to juggle it all, we get stressed. We want our kids to excel in life. If they have a talent, of course we do our best to nurture it. There's nothing more satisfying than having happy children who are living to their full potential. It would be strange if we didn't want to bless our kids. After all, we rocked them to sleep in the middle of the night, kissed their skinned knees, disciplined them, bought them presents, and protected them from danger. We *should* want the best for our kids.

Sports, unfortunately, takes the idea of best to an all new level. As our kids grow older and the competition gets tougher, even the most laid-back parents fight insomnia, bitterness, and anger at times.

Part of the problem is our expectations for our kids grow higher as we're becoming vulnerable in our own lives. Wrinkles have popped up overnight. Gray hairs, too. Life isn't one big adventure anymore—if it ever was. The career we busted our tails for? Not as fulfilling as we'd hoped. The body we used to have? Takes a lot more work to keep in shape than it used to. The money troubles we thought would be long gone? Still there with no end in sight.

If doubts wriggle in about sports—*can we afford it? Is this team good for him? Should she drop volleyball to have more time for homework?*—we shush the pesky whispers. Hopping off the merry-go-round of sports? Sounds like a fantasy— one that will end with our kid the loser. Quitting a sport doesn't even seem like an option, not when our child has come this far.

Yes, we have a lot riding on our children. We look at them and see possibilities no longer viable for us.

And we want them to have the life we dreamed about but didn't quite get.

Giving Them Something Better

Maybe we hope, as the media suggests, that excelling in sports will ensure our kids end up with confidence, success, and happiness. In the back of our minds we believe being athletes will guarantee our children obtain the dream life.

Why do we believe excelling in a sport is the key to our kids' confidence, success, and happiness? Is it because we've put professional athletes on a pedestal? Some of these players are positive role models, but the news is full of stories about sports' heroes behaving badly. And it isn't all sunbeams and roses for the pros. Professional athletes get injured, travel constantly during the season, fear being traded to another team with little or no say in the matter, tiptoe through a new set of hassles related to their wealth, and face extremely short careers. The dream life? Is rare to achieve and comes with a price.

We squirm a little when anyone questions our motives regarding sports. After all, our children show so much promise. Besides, we're raising them with morals, and who said anything about going pro? Our babies will play sports and breeze through life. The negatives only apply to other kids, older athletes.

Are we sure about that?

Our kids *can* live with integrity and be high-level athletes. But we need to guide them, and the lines get blurred the further up they climb.

After those early years of juice boxes and crackers, players begin to stand out. They try out for competitive teams. We want our children to have the same opportunities as their peers. When their friends move up, we look to the future and wonder who will have a better chance at clinching a varsity spot on the high school team or earning an athletic scholarship to a university. We feel compelled to provide our kids with experiences that will be advantageous to them.

Did you notice the two new additions that snuck onto the list of reasons our kids play sports? Yes, making the varsity team and getting a college scholarship are now part of our narrative. These two little gems become permanently etched on the list somewhere between enrolling Susie in private tennis lessons and dragging Johnny to the all-star soccer team tryouts.

We're motivated to have our children play sports for many reasons, and not all of them are obvious. Like licking through layers of a jawbreaker, when we get honest with ourselves, we find the heart of the matter, the truth, the good stuff.

My good stuff was hiding beneath several layers of decoys and a thick crust of anxiety, but I found it when I asked the following question.

What did I want my kids to get out of sports?

After listing the socially acceptable reasons—nurturing their talents, keeping them in shape, having a better chance at playing in high school—I realized the core of my thinking went much deeper. I didn't want my kids to play sports just to develop their talents or to make a high school team.

I wanted more for them.

I wanted sports to help my children become their best possible selves.

I wanted them to learn how to play on a team, how to win, how to lose, how to fail, how to be kind, how to be confident, how to toughen up, and most importantly, how to grow up to be mature adults. Essentially, I hoped sports would help my kids become good people.

When I understood my motivations, my actions and reactions changed.

Our approach to sports directly affects our children. As parents we have a much greater responsibility than just driving them to and from practices, paying fees, and giving them pointers or pep talks.

We need to show our kids how to live with integrity because they are so much more than the sport they play.

Your child is more than an athlete. Your child is God's child, a light in this world.

Society says only winners matter.

God says anyone who believes in Him matters. According to John 3:16, "For God so loved the world that he gave his one and only Son, that whoever believes in him shall not perish but have eternal life."

Society says do what's right for you.

God says submit to Him. Proverbs 3:5-6 states, "Trust in the Lord with all your heart and lean not on your own understanding; in all your ways submit to him and he will make your paths straight."

Win or submit? Winning sounds better, right?

Not when it means losing what's most important to you.

Trusting God to make our paths straight isn't always easy, especially when we're on the sidelines watching players take the court while our equally talented son sits on the bench. Again. At that moment, we're not thinking about how this will help him become a stronger person. And when our daughter misses a soccer goal, it's hard to accept that this might be a time she has to learn how to fail. When we watch parents engage in politics that directly hurt our children, we'd do just about anything to prevent them from learning this particular lesson on how the world works.

Competitive sports can be an ugly place. The ugliness isn't only reserved for older players. It's there at all ages, and it makes me sad.

There are many negatives in competitive sports that parents can't change, but I don't believe the answer is to avoid sports altogether. For many of us, sports are a permanent part of our kids' lives, and the benefits outweigh the drawbacks.

This is why it's vital to spend time figuring out why *you* want your kids to play. My reasons won't be the same as yours. But when I clarified why I allowed my children to play sports, I changed. And when you clarify it for yourself, you will, too.

Oh, I still become the princess of darkness occasionally. I still get overly enthusiastic wanting my kids to do their best. Still bristle at injustices, get disgusted by politics, and get angry at unfairness. But I no longer put sports on a pedestal. This has made a tremendous difference in my life by freeing me to be the parent my kids need.

How Will This Affect Their Future?

When I went on my quest to understand why we had our kids in sports, I kept coming back to one question. Years from now, what did I want my children to remember about playing?

When they are all grown up, I hope their memories include bonding as a team, pushing themselves to try harder, having fun, brushing off mistakes, laughing with their friends, supporting their teammates, and gaining confidence in their abilities.

I hope their answers don't include worrying about letting my husband and I down, feeling like the worst player on the team, hating the sport because it was too much pressure, being heckled by teammates or other parents, constantly being screamed at by a coach, or feeling as if they could never live up to our expectations.

Parents have chances at every game, on the way to and from every practice, throughout the off-season, and during tryouts to influence their kids' thoughts and behaviors for good or for bad. We are their role models. They see how we act, hear what we say, and they feel our approval, insecurity, or anger.

Children are influenced by the people they spend the most time with. Young players typically look up to their parents more than their peers and coaches because they are around us more. They want to please us. They want to make us proud.

And sadly, for some kids, no matter how hard they work, it isn't enough to make their parents proud. Nothing they do will ever be enough. They feel as if they're only as good as their last game.

If you're reading this with a sinking feeling, don't worry. It's not too late to be the parent you want to be. You can start modeling the behavior you want your kids to imitate.

It's never too late to mentally put sports in their proper place.

This is the book I wish I'd owned when our children made their debuts in sports. It's the guide I continue to turn to each season whenever pride, insecurity, and unhealthy competitiveness sneak in. I need it today. I'll need it tomorrow. Why? Because simmering just below the surface of youth sports is a lie. And it's easy to buy into.

Truths to Take Away:

1. Not all kids play sports for the same reason. Think about why you want your children in sports. Dig deep to get to the heart of it. Are your words and actions backing up your reasons? Or have pride, insecurity, and unhealthy competitiveness crept in?

2. Kids are influenced by their parents' actions. What kind of people do you want your children to grow up to be? Do your words and actions regarding sports reflect this?

3. Our kids will grow up. When they do, what do you want them to remember about sports?

CHAPTER TWO

Don't Believe The Lie

"I praise you because I am fearfully and wonderfully made; your works are wonderful, I know that full well." Psalm 139:14 (NIV)

Susie dives into the pool. Her head emerges from the water several inches ahead of the girl in the lane next to her. Susie's strokes are powerful, and she expertly turns at the other end of the pool. She's in the lead. Your heart races as she nears the finish. *Come on, come on!* And then she touches the wall.

She won!

You jump up and down, cheering, then text your best friend the good news. This is the best day ever! It feels so good—it's almost as if you won, too!

Their Win Is Your Win

This wonderful moment is often where the lie takes root. What lie is that?

We begin to equate our kids' success with our own. This is the heart of why so many parents are stressed out about sports. Don't get me wrong, we should be proud of our children's accomplishments but not if that rush of pride is for all the wrong reasons.

When we equate our children's success with our own, we become emotionally invested in an unhealthy way. Lurking undetected beneath a personal lifetime of highs and lows sits the sense of a do-over. Although we know our pasts can't be changed, we thrust our kids into roles they shouldn't have to play—the role of fulfilling our washed-up dreams or avoiding our failures.

Maybe you were a star athlete in school and know firsthand how it can raise a teen's social status. You're relieved your son will have the same advantages you enjoyed, and you don't mind the boost in your own status as the parent of an important player.

Or you could have been the kid stumbling over his feet in gym class, left out of the accolades at the annual sports banquet. Your son won't have to feel inferior to the jocks because he'll be one of them. Plus, this is your chance to finally be included, albeit from the sidelines.

Maybe you were the girl desperate to make the cheerleading squad except your parents couldn't afford the pricey tumbling classes necessary to make the team. You vowed your daughter would have the chances you were denied, and her spot as a cheerleader feels like your lost spot.

Years after our own sports' dramas have concluded, we heave a sigh of relief that our son or daughter might be better equipped at surviving those turbulent teen years.

We want our children to live up to our expectations, but our expectations can be warped. It feels amazing when they succeed, but what happens when they're benched? Injured? Have a bad game?

Unfortunately, the lie goes both ways. We also equate our kids' failure as our own.

Our emotions become directly tied to how our kids perform. If our son scores the winning touchdown, we feel like we scored, too. But a week later when he drops the ball and sits out the rest of the game, we're disappointed, maybe even embarrassed.

Feelings of winning are strong, and we want them repeated. Feelings of losing are even more powerful, and we'll go to great lengths to avoid them. We get too caught up in the right-here-and-now and lose sight of why they're playing the game in the first place.

When our self-worth gets tied up with how our kids perform, everyone suffers. If our daughter has a bad game, we can no longer be the adult she needs because our egos took a hit, too. Instead of seeing the long-term reasons she's playing, we're upset. And we want her problem fixed. Right now. On the flip side, if she's the star player, we forget to be humble, forget that positions and skill levels are liquid, changing every year.

If I've taken away anything as a parent with children in competitive sports, it's this. How my kids perform should have no effect on my self-worth. Zero. None.

My children are *not* better than anyone else when they excel at sports. My children are *not* worse than anyone else when they struggle at sports.

And I'm not better or worse than any other parent when my kids excel or struggle.

We can't get our self-worth from how our kids perform. We must work hard at checking our emotions when it comes to sports.

Our kids are watching us. They pick up on our hopes, our disappointments, our insecurities. The last impression we want to give them is that their worth as human beings is based on their performances on the field.

And, really, shouldn't *our worth* be based on more than their performances, too?

As simple as it is to say, "Don't believe the lie," putting it into practice can be difficult. It's easy to get caught up in winning and to react poorly when losing.

Strategies To Combat The Lie

Since I don't want my self-worth tied up with my children's sports, I had to figure out what my self-worth *should* be based on. I grabbed a pen and paper and thought about my accomplishments. What had I done that I was proud of? What could I cling to the next time I found myself hijacking one of their successes or failures?

It took me a while to come up with a list. My life hasn't been filled with flashy wins. As I reflected back, I realized my greatest accomplishments didn't come with trophies or accolades. In fact, the things that make me most proud are behaviors I've honed over the years. Persistence, being organized, choosing kindness over spitefulness, striving to be humble. Honestly, I consider making dinner for our family every night a major achievement.

Think about what you've accomplished in life. What are you proud of? What do you do well? Write down five things. This might come extremely easy to you, but don't worry if you're stumped. Surprisingly, this exercise can be difficult. It was for me!

Try to focus on qualities and skills you've developed. Are you great at planning birthday parties, the person friends come to when they need a shoulder to cry on, the one always willing to donate time for causes you believe in, or the rock who keeps your family feeling normal during a crisis?

Regardless of what you write down, the point is to understand that *you matter*. Yes, you. The things you do, even if they seem tiny in your eyes, are important. You don't have to win awards or have some unique skill set to be vital in someone's life. The everyday things you do make a difference. When you show up to work every morning, you're providing food and shelter for your family. When you hug your daughter at night and tell her you love her, you make the world a better place. Do you think she cares you won a bowling trophy thirteen years ago? She cares more about the way you make her feel, so the hugs and the time you spend with her are vital.

Your son's hockey career is not as important as you're making it out to be. Your daughter's position on the lacrosse team isn't either. The worries gripping you—*will he get benched? Will she even make the team next year? Why doesn't the coach see that she's better than so-and-so? Why did he break his arm?*—will not matter five years from now.

You might be thinking, *my son's hockey career is important. He's already gotten a scholarship to play for a Big Ten university.* That's great, but it isn't going to guarantee he'll grow into a mature adult with morals. Celebrate his work ethic or his good sportsmanship, but please, don't put all the emphasis on his position with the team. He could get injured. He could be replaced by someone else. And he should still be worthy of praise in your eyes.

You're worthy of praise, too. Maybe your parents never valued you. Maybe you're disenchanted with your adult relationships. Being a grown-up is hard.

Rest assured you have a Father in heaven who cherishes you. Psalm 139:13-14 sums it up, "For you created my inmost being; you knit me together in my mother's womb. I praise you because I am wonderfully and fearfully made; your works are wonderful. I know that full well."

We don't need to get our self-worth from our children. We are wonderfully and fearfully made. Nothing can change that.

Our children's self-worth shouldn't come from sports either. They shouldn't feel as if they're only as good as their last game.

With that being said, it's time to focus on the ways our kids make us proud. We've looked at our own accomplishments and behaviors. Now list five ways each of your children makes you proud that aren't related to sports. Maybe your son is an excellent reader. Your daughter is always kind to the neighbor two doors down. Your youngest makes people laugh with his quick wit. Your oldest never has to be told to do her homework.

This exercise was much easier for me than listing my own accomplishments. I could list pages and pages of why I'm proud of my kids.

Maybe you're wondering why you should do these exercises. Can't you just read this book and move on? Yes, but identifying your accomplishments gives you something concrete to reflect on when you're stressed at a game. And reminding yourself that sports are just one part of your children's lives can take the edge off during the tough times.

Knowing we shouldn't internalize our kids' successes and failures doesn't always translate to us behaving rationally. Sports can consume our lives. That's why I had to get brutally honest with myself.

What qualities did I want my children to develop? Were my words and actions in line with these goals?

I want them to become trustworthy, faith-filled, patient, hard-working, honest, kind, loving adults. I don't want to raise self-centered, critical, entitled, lazy, unethical people. Who does?

Unfortunately, we don't always *show* our kids the traits we want them to have. They watch what we do and hear what we say. If we don't want them to become entitled adults, then we shouldn't demand special treatment for them now. Our job is to help them develop their self-esteems by emphasizing the qualities we want them to develop while minimizing our desire for them to be recognized as special. And it isn't always easy.

Truths to Take Away:

1. My children are valuable for who they are not because of their positions in sports.

2. My kids do not have to be perfect. They are allowed to have good games and bad games, tough seasons and great seasons.

3. My self-worth should not be tied to how my children perform in sports.

4. We were fearfully and wonderfully made by God. We are worth so much more than we know!

CHAPTER THREE

You Will Feel Anxiety

"Do not be anxious about anything, but in every situation, by prayer and petition, with thanksgiving, present your requests to God."
Philippians 4:6 (NIV)

Sports are anxiety producers of a high order for parents. For a long time I believed that the older my kids became, the less stress I would feel. Actually, the stress gets worse. Every year it's worse. And it's not just me. Many parents with kids on competitive teams deal with anxiety throughout the season.

Anxiety Kick-Starters

- Your daughter gets a new position. Will she be good at it?

- The team is winning. What if they blow it and lose?
- The team is losing. They're falling apart.
- Your son misses a key play. Oh, no! Everyone will blame him.
- A parent heckles your child. How dare she?
- The official makes a bad call. Stupid ref...
- Weather issues. How can anyone kick a ball in this hurricane?
- Injuries. She'll lose her position if she doesn't heal soon.
- Illness. But practices are mandatory...
- Money. How will we scrape up the cash for uniforms and fees?
- Scheduling conflicts. So Susie has dance class across town, Johnny needs to be at the lacrosse field, and, wait—who's going to pick up Annie from track?

Anything can produce anxiety. Even the tiny things. Your daughter accidentally forgot her knee pads. You left the cooler full of drinks in the garage. Your toddler needs a nap, but you can't miss the game. You have no cash on hand, and the tournament entrance fee is five dollars per person. Thankfully, the little anxieties are short-lived.

The bigger issues, though, cause long-term anxiety, and they're usually tied to performance.

When your child is performing well, you breathe easier. Cheering for the team comes naturally. You don't dread games; you look forward to them.

But when your child is struggling, doesn't have the position he deserves, or is being picked on by teammates, coaches, or other parents, your muscles tense. Cheering? Who can cheer through this torture? You might even envy the parents with scheduling conflicts, the ones who are missing this game to be at a different event.

Yes, anxiety can eat you alive. I know. I've been there. I'm still there sometimes.

So we have the short-term anxieties, the long-term ones and let's add a new one—the am-I-a-bad-parent worry. We don't have much control over sports, and we question if we're doing the right thing. Should Johnny try out for a different travel team? What if Susie makes the B team instead of the A team? We really can't afford three hundred dollars a month for competitive cheer, but Annie's coach thinks she's special. If we say no to this team are we ending Johnny's athletic future?

We can't see how it will all work out, and if it doesn't end the way we'd hoped, we feel like bad parents.

Dealing With The Pressure

How can we deal with all of this pressure? First of all, recognize it comes with the territory. We don't need to be held hostage by the what-ifs of sports. We have someone we can always turn to, and we should.

God loves us. He loves our kids. He's here, taking care of us, caring about us. This is spelled out in 1 Peter 5:7, "Cast all your anxiety on him because he cares for you." Prayer won't take away all of our problems, but it helps us get perspective.

Also, remember, no kid is perfect. Every player on the team will struggle with something during the season. You aren't the only parents sacrificing financially. You also aren't the only ones with scheduling problems, anxiety about your child's performance, worries about positions and coaches and everything else.

I often remind myself the highs and lows are normal.

We don't know the big picture. We don't know God's plan in all of this. We get caught up in the here-and-now—scores, stats, bragging rights—but the Lord looks at the heart. Maybe God is teaching your son or daughter something valuable. Maybe He's teaching *you* something valuable. What looks like failure or disappointment to us could be the turning point for our child to develop a rock-solid confidence. The missed play results in a teammate encouraging your daughter, showing her she's valued. Or, maybe another player yells about the missed play, and that night your daughter cries about it until you remind her that the team wins and loses together. Rebounding from pain builds perseverance.

Life lessons.

Anxiety.

At times it's exhilarating to watch our kids play sports. Other times, it's excruciating. Yes, we'll feel anxiety, but we don't have to let it rule our lives.

When Your Anxiety Becomes Excessive

It's easy for me to say overcoming difficulties produces perseverance and confidence. When you're sitting in the stands and your kid is smack dab in the middle of a bad season, it's nearly impossible to focus on the life lessons your child may or may not be learning. You just want the situation to improve. Anxiety rushes in and gets worse the longer the rough patch lasts.

WHAT ARE THE SIGNS YOUR ANXIETY HAS REACHED A TIPPING POINT?

- You can't sleep at night. Maybe you're worried because Johnny got demoted to second string. Will he ever get his spot back? Or politics outside of your control are directly affecting his playing time. You seethe and toss and turn and know you need to rest, but you can't relax.
- Every thought of the team brings up rage or bitterness based on how your child is being treated.
- If someone asks about your child's sport, you launch into an unholy rant with a lengthy list of grievances. This doesn't soothe your anger. It intensifies it.
- You're obsessively trying to fix your child's weak spots.
- You can barely watch your kid play because your stomach is tied in knots.
- You're consumed with what-ifs. What if we wouldn't have pushed her to try out for this team? What if we would have investigated a different team? What if we were wrong for making her choose one sport? What if I wouldn't have said that stupid thing to the coach? What if...?
- The sport is a hot zone topic in your household, and neither you nor your spouse can mention it without tempers flaring.
- Your child was considered the best player last season. What if she's no longer able to perform at a top level?

- You expect the worst to happen at any given moment, and you don't know what the worst is, but it sure feels like Armageddon.

I've been there. I'm not proud of it. I've come up with some simple strategies to lessen my anxiety. Can we eliminate worrying completely? Some of you may be able to, but I doubt it's in my DNA.

STRATEGIES TO LESSON THE ANXIETY

1) Try to pinpoint the exact reason you're stressed out about the sport. Is it a sense of unfairness? Is it the fear that your kid really isn't as good as the other players? Is it insecurity about possibly having to switch teams next season?

2) Ask yourself what's the worst that can happen?
   Here are some possibilities.
   What if...
   a. Your kid is benched?
   She's still your darling daughter. Go back to the list you wrote of your child's accomplishments. Tell her why you're proud of her, and let her know she'll get through this.
   b. Your kid gets cut from the team next year?
   He might want to play on another team where he'll get more playing time or a different position. He might want to try another sport. Or, in fantasy-land, he'll take up jogging and you'll get free time!

c. The dad scheming for his daughter to take your baby's spot succeeds?
This is an area you don't have much control over. You can have her try out for a different team, and you won't have to be around that parent anymore. Or you can have your daughter stick it out, work hard, and hope the coach rewards her for it.

d. Your kid misses a key play, causing the team to lose?
Oh, well. It happens in every sport, every season, all across the world. These are games. Games have winners and losers. Sometimes your kid will be responsible for the final losing play. Sometimes your child will be responsible for the final winning play. It's just how it goes.

e. Your kid gets concussion number three?
Look, if your son never plays sports again, he will still have a wonderful life. Plenty of children DO NOT play sports, and they grow up fine.

3) Remind yourself the season won't last forever. We have almost no control over playing time, positions, the way teammates perceive our kids, injuries, and so on. Why waste time getting worked up about things we can't control? All we can do is make wise decisions based on the information we have and pray for the best.

4) Instead of being a throbbing ball of worry on the bleachers, make an effort with the other parents. Talk to them. Cheer for their kids. If possible, be a positive person out there. If it's not possible, try to stay quiet. Be the role

model your kids need. Who knows, maybe you'll encourage other parents who are anxious, too.

5) Off-season, weigh your options. Is this team good for my child? We may not like it, but adversity grows character. It won't destroy our kid if he isn't the favorite, nor will it kill his confidence if he has to deal with a few jerks. However, if there are too many toxic teammates and parents, carefully consider if this is where he needs to be. Does he seem depressed? Have you noticed personality changes? Has he lost his desire to attend practices or games? Any appetite changes? Do your family a favor and either find a different team or take a season off.

6) Pray through it all. Pray for guidance. Pray for wisdom. And pray for peace.

Anxiety doesn't have to be a permanent part of each season. Try different strategies to combat stress. You'll be so glad you did.

Truths to Take Away:

1. Anxiety is always lurking if your kid is in a sport.

2. Anxiety gets worse when your child is in the middle of a learning season. What looks like failure could be the factor that gives your kid the determination to try harder and consequently grow stronger.

3. We might not be able to control how our kids perform, but we can control how we respond.

CHAPTER FOUR

Character Matters

When I began writing this book, one thing that stood out for me was character. My goal has always been to raise kids with morals who work hard and live with integrity. Playing sports seemed to support this. After all, they're striving to meet their potential. They're trying to be the best. We, as parents, celebrate this. The problem with putting so much emphasis on our kids being the best is that they find ways to get to the top even if it doesn't build their characters.

What Kind Of Adults Do You Want Your Children To Become?

I looked up the noun, *character,* in a few dictionaries and found several definitions with references to integrity, firmness, reputation, and moral excellence.[1]

I see a lot of firmness in sports. Some kids have quiet strength and others have swagger. Both can be good. I believe it's beneficial and necessary to own our successes as we work hard toward a goal. But some kids are under the impression that swagger means acting superior to everyone. They simply can't handle being considered anything less than number one on the team.

We don't always realize we reinforce this attitude. When another player competes for our kid's position, we're tempted to criticize him. We knowingly or unknowingly pit our child against another by telling him to fight for his position or by criticizing the player. This creates a breeding ground for arrogance and insecurity.

How can our children develop integrity? Playing on a team provides plenty of opportunities for them to make moral decisions. I'm not only talking about big issues. Kids have a choice when a teammate misses the ball. Our daughter can ridicule the girl or pat her on the back and tell her she'll get it next time. Players choose whether to put in maximum effort at practices or to goof off when the coach isn't watching. Our son can decide to clean up after himself or let someone else pick up his empty water bottles. Our kids should take responsibility for their mistakes and not blame circumstances or other people.

Sports are equally capable of pushing our children to take the easier, less-moral path. These shortcuts only develop self-entitlement or victim mentalities. I'm convinced insecurity skyrockets when kids take the easy way out.

Insecurity fuels many problems in sports today. It also plays a huge role in how parents react to their kids' sports. Not only are the players themselves insecure—*what if I don't make the team? What if I do make the team, but I don't get the position I want? What if the coach doesn't like me? What if I drop the ball/miss the goal/lose the game?*—parents are insecure too. For identical reasons.

Insecurity doesn't only affect kids. It leads parents to fret, which prods them to scheme to ensure their kids get more playing time, better positions, or anything else on their worry list. Scheming for our children robs them of opportunities to develop integrity.

How Would You React?

Let's say your son was a star player on the B travel soccer team last year, but this year he tries out for the A team and earns a spot. You and your spouse are convinced the A team will be good for him. He'll play against harder teams. He'll also have some bragging rights—not that he'll brag—that he's good enough to play upper level. Plus, he'll have a better chance to play on the high school team.

Midway through the season on the A team, he's no longer pumped about going to practice. In fact, he's starting to say that he hates soccer, that it's stupid. You wonder if he misses the bond with his old teammates. He thrived with them. You've been frustrated this season, too. He's not getting as much playing time as some of the other players. You start to question if the coach has favorites. Is that why your son isn't playing more?

You want to solve the problem, but you don't know how. You ask your son why he's upset. He says the coach has favorites, and he's tired of sitting on the bench.

Favorites? Just what you thought.

So what do you do about it?

Reaction 1: You might get on the phone with the coach and accuse him (subtly or outright) of playing favorites. You demand more playing time for your son. As the result of this conversation, maybe the coach gives him more playing time, or maybe he doesn't.

At upcoming games, whenever your son is on the bench, he reverts to his moody, glum self. You hate seeing him unhappy, and it isn't fair so many kids play entire games while other players only get a few minutes here or there. How can he prove himself if he never plays? And how can he get better sitting on the bench?

When tryouts come around next year, your son shrugs and says he doesn't want to play anymore. You're convinced it's because of the coach, so you have him try out for another team. Problem solved! Until he sits on the bench. He's right back in gloomy, blaming mode.

The consequences?

Both parent and child acted out of insecurity. When you asked your son what was wrong, he confirmed your initial assumption. Maybe the coach *was* playing favorites. But when you demanded more playing time from the coach, your son learned that his effort didn't matter. If he doesn't like what life throws at him, Mom and Dad will fix it.

This robs him of learning the valuable skill of fighting through adversity. Pouting and a poor attitude got your son special treatment (the phone call to the coach) and an excuse to continue feeling sorry for himself (it's not his fault he's not playing more).

But maybe you're shaking your head. It's not that you wanted special treatment; you wanted your kid to be treated *fairly* and to get *equal playing time*. Unless your son is on a league that ensures equal playing time, you can't demand it. Frankly, sports are rarely fair, and playing time is never equal.

Reaction 2: When you ask your son what's wrong and he says the coach is playing favorites, you concede it's possible. You then ask your son additional questions. Is he practicing as hard as he can? Has the coach mentioned any areas he needs to work on?

At this point, your son gets defensive. Of course, he's working hard. Coach likes the starters the best. Your son might start to claim that he's "not good at soccer." The conversation deteriorates, and you're not sure how to move forward.

Maybe you call the coach, but instead of demanding more playing time, you ask if anything has been going on at practices you aren't aware of. Is your son goofing off? Is there anything he's struggling with? Do the players get along?

Or you don't call the coach. You might refrain because you're convinced he *is* playing favorites, doesn't see your son's talent, and no amount of phone calls will change that. On the other hand, you might not call because you refuse to interfere.

Regardless of whether you call the coach or not, you encourage your son to give one hundred percent effort at practices, to be respectful, and to make the most of every opportunity out on the field. You also assure him he made the team for a reason, that he earned his spot.

He sighs. Grumbles. The next couple of weeks are the same. He's clearly not enjoying his non-starter status, but on the rare occasions when the coach puts him in, he does well and joy lights up his face. You applaud his hard work. He still isn't a starter, but he's less negative about practices.

His season doesn't improve. There isn't a Hollywood ending to this one. But by the final game, he no longer wants to quit the sport. He might not handle every setback with grace, and he still will have his pouty moments as his career progresses, but you see a core of strength that had been lacking previously.

The consequences?

If you asked him what changed over the season to help him go from wanting to quit to enjoying the sport again, he probably wouldn't be able to give you an exact answer. You might not know the answer either.

Deep down the experience taught him that being a top player on the team isn't the most important part of his soccer life. He is starting to develop perseverance. His confidence grows because in his heart he knows he practiced hard and did his best. Whether the coach recognized his talent or not, your son was forced to believe in himself when no one was patting him on the back or even trusting his ability to contribute to the team.

He has become more resilient.

And you have, too.

Why is reaction one so familiar to many parents, while reaction two is much harder for parents to choose?

My husband and I believe in being honest with our kids. We don't gloss over the realities of life. If they feel an injustice by other players or their coach, we listen and don't assume they're imagining things. However, we don't foster an environment of blaming others or being victims. We encourage them to work hard and to do their personal best.

Not the coach's favorite? Practice as hard as you can. Sitting on the bench more than the other kids? Do your best when you *are* put in the game. Think you're a better player than so-and-so? Who cares? Make the most of the opportunities that come your way instead of envying and criticizing another player or the coach.

Creating Problems By Fixing Everything

Character is developed when we face difficulties. When we let our children dwell in the uncomfortable, they develop qualities to rise above it. When we do everything we can to eliminate discomfort for them, they don't develop the inner strength needed in life. They learn that being uncomfortable should be avoided at all costs. They either rely on Mom and Dad to fix their problems, they cheat, or they quit.

Another way insecurity can hurt our child's character is by giving her an inflated sense of self. Seems like a contradiction, doesn't it?

When your kid is struggling at an aspect of a sport, you might over-praise her or go the opposite way and constantly harp on her weaknesses. Both can confuse her to the point she no longer has a rational view of her strengths and weaknesses. This can lead her to criticize teammates while ignoring her own questionable skills.

Kids can be brutal. If your child complains about a teammate, remind her that being part of a team is supporting everyone on it. With that in mind, try your best not to bad-mouth another player in front of her. A divided team isn't good for anyone.

One thing I'm not great at is simply listening to my children. I try to let them vent about whatever is bothering them without getting defensive or going into fix-it mode, but more times than not, I fail. I have to remind myself they can handle their problems on their own. If I don't go into panic mode, my kids realize the issue isn't as huge as they are making it out to be, and they're more likely to get over it faster.

Sometimes I ask them questions to help them think situations through. I also try to empathize by putting myself in their shoes, not as the adult me, but as me at their ages. It helps to think back when I was ten or twelve or fourteen. Trust me, I didn't have it all together back then! So why would I expect my kid to at the same age?

The Showboat Wins

You might be shaking your head right now. Kids don't learn to be aggressive by passively taking what life gives them.

Well, it's pretty obvious to me that the aggressive kids get the most playing time and tend to be favored by the coaches. But it's equally obvious that the most aggressive kids are not always the players with the highest skill levels. They believe they're the best because they're treated as if they are. This doesn't translate to actual talent. They put on a good show and are rewarded for it. And because of this, they get an overinflated impression of their skills.

The most talented players are often the under-the-radar players. They're the ones who actually make the baskets, catch the football and run it in for a touchdown, set teammates up to score, and play great defense while the more aggressive players get so caught up in being big shots, they trip over their own feet trying to kick a goal. Because the aggressive players look like they are trying hard, they continue to get the best positions, whereas the quieter kids are often undervalued on a team.

Yes, the showboats usually win at youth sports. Their confidence soars, coaches and kids admire them, and their parents bask in the glow of their star player. But as these kids grow older, they don't always settle down enough to hone their skills. They rely on showmanship over substance. In higher level sports, they struggle to compete mentally and physically against more poised players.

If your sole goal is to have your child be the star player now, than by all means, ignore this segment on character. But if you want your kid to grow into a valuable player as well as a person with integrity, emphasize substance over style.

I'd love to say that all coaches encourage kids to play in a way that builds character. However, coaches are as competitive as the next person.

They want to win. Some of them are very good role models. Others flat out force kids to cheat. If your child is on a team where cheating is encouraged or required, please remove her. Immediately. You do not want her tarnished by that mentality.

Yes, character matters. Even when it's difficult, let's try to encourage our children to develop moral excellence, to work hard, and to handle their problems on their own. One day they'll grow up, and they'll pass these lessons on to their kids. The next generation will need it as much as the current one. The world is a very competitive place, and that won't change anytime soon.

Truths to Take Away:

1. Kids are learning more than physical skills on sports' teams. They are learning how to handle disappointments, how to support people who might not deserve it, how to deal with a loss, and how to act after a win. Encourage and reward behavior that builds moral excellence.

2. Life isn't fair. We don't need to pretend it is. But pushing our weight around to get special treatment for our kids does not build their character. They need to develop skills to get through life's ups and downs. Allow them to be uncomfortable when faced with problems, and give them emotional support at home.

3. Confidence is built after facing adversity. If you solve all your kids' problems, you rob them of the chance to build true confidence.

4. Acting superior to others is arrogance, not confidence.

CHAPTER FIVE

The World Is More Competitive

"The fear of the LORD is the beginning of knowledge, but fools despise wisdom and instruction." Proverbs 1:7 (NIV)

When my kids were young, I lived in a blissful imaginary world where elite teams and year-round practices weren't expected or required to break into a high school sport. In my mind, if you wanted to play a sport in high school and had a smidgeon of talent, you'd be fine.

How wrong I was.

Our six-year-old daughter had just spent two years in dance and wanted to learn how to tumble, so we enrolled her in a local gymnastics facility. While she walked backwards on the balance beam, I chatted with a few other moms in the waiting area. We could see the entire gym. I remember thinking how tiny the girls looked in their leotards. One mom with a daughter in the same class mentioned that her little girl would be starting Level 1 the following year.

Level 1? What's that?

It involved two-hour practices three days a week. Competing in showcases. And it cost a lot of money to pay for the classes, leotards, and travel fees.

Yikes! Three days a week? Two hours a night? And showcases? But my little girl is in first grade. Isn't that a bit much?

My mind was closing the door on the topic until the real kicker dropped. The mom mentioned *future college scholarships.*

I went home and mulled the conversation over, talked to my husband about it, and we decided our daughter was too young for that kind of pressure and time commitment. Unfortunately, she was no longer able to take lessons because the gym didn't offer recreational classes beyond beginner gymnastics. Unless she moved into Level 1, she was out.

It all became as clear to me as a glass of purified water. Wait too long to get your kids involved in the sport of their choice, and they won't have a chance to compete with their peers who started as young children. This theory was confirmed time and again as both of our kids grew older and were involved in a variety of activities.

Sports, as I had known them, had changed.

I could not find accurate data regarding how many kids participate in sports today as opposed to ten, twenty, or thirty years ago. However, data is available online for individual sports.

Let's look at the extremely popular youth sport of soccer. US Youth Soccer has recreational teams and competitive teams for children ages 5-19.[2] According to US Youth Soccer's "Key Statistics,"[3] the US Youth Soccer Annual Registration of Players swelled from 810,793 players in 1980 to 3,055,148 players in 2014. That's an increase of over 375% in 34 years.

Were three million kids playing soccer in 1980? Maybe. But if they were, over two million of them weren't playing on teams recognized by US Youth Soccer.

Pick a sport, and you're likely to find similar statistics with the exception of sports such as baseball that have a longer history of organized leagues.

Basically, kids have been playing a variety of sports throughout the years, but more kids today play on competitive teams affiliated with organized leagues than they did in the past.

Recreational Vs. Competitive Teams

Recreational? Competitive? Wait, aren't all teams competitive?

For brevity's sake, I'm calling all teams that hold tryouts competitive teams. These include tournament teams, all-star teams, travel teams, and any other name they might go by. Competitive teams are usually part of a larger organization and play against other teams within that organization who adhere to the same rules.

Recreational teams, on the other hand, allow any child to be on the roster, regardless of their skill level. They are usually part of a local parks and recreation program or an association such as the YMCA.

Recreational teams tend to be coached by parents, some of whom played in high school or college and others with limited, if any, experience with the sport. Rec sports emphasize having fun (although from my experience, some are more fun than others), and kids are supposed to have equal playing time (again, the words *supposed to* don't always apply—it depends on the team). Rec teams will have a mixture of beginners and more advanced players.

Competitive teams expect their players to be proficient; therefore, they hold tryouts. They typically charge fees and hold mandatory practices in addition to the games. They might require travel and year-round practices. The coaches are usually parents of players on the team, but these coaches have experience at a higher level—high school, college, or above.

Whether you choose recreational teams or competitive teams for your child to play on is up to you. As your kid grows older, you'll have to weigh the pros and cons of each. Here are some factors to consider.

Rec teams typically have fewer practices and shorter seasons. Kids of all skill levels will play together. The coaches may teach proper techniques, or they might not even know proper techniques. Your kid might learn how to do things the wrong way, or you might be fortunate enough to have coaches who teach them the correct methods. The teams your kids face will be similar to theirs—with some good players and some less talented ones. The costs will be minimal. No matter how much emphasis is put on "fun," parents will take the game seriously.

On the other hand, competitive teams have more practices—sometimes year-round—and longer seasons. The coaches will know proper techniques and teach them accordingly. The kids on the team will be at a comparable skill level. The opponents they face will have rosters of kids at similar talent levels. Some teams will be more elite than others. The costs vary but can be quite pricey. Again, parents will take the game seriously. Whatever type of team you choose—recreational or competitive—be prepared for parents taking the game seriously!

What Age Should Kids Begin Sports?

Recreational teams are available for children as young as three years old. Competitive teams begin later, depending on the sport. For instance, the earliest age to try out for a competitive baseball team is typically eight years old, but many areas do not offer competitive baseball until kids are nine or ten. You'll have to check your area for the specifics of the sport you're considering.

Keep in mind that regardless of the type of team, children are starting organized sports at young ages. Does your kid have to play basketball at five-years-old? Of course not. Some sports can be pursued down the line. For instance, volleyball skills do not need to be drilled into a six-year-old. Ditto for football. However, some sports *do* require a commitment at a young age.

If your daughter has any desire to compete in gymnastics, you'll need to enroll her in a program when she's quite young. There's nothing wrong with signing a twelve-year-old up for gymnastics, but don't expect her to compete with other twelve-year-olds who have been training daily and competing year-round for five to six years.

I hope as your children grow older, they want to try different sports. Our kids tried many activities throughout the years, and we still encourage them to try something new if it interests them. That's what life is about.

A word of caution. Please, do not try to force your children to play a sport because you love

it. They will be the ones playing—let them decide if they want to try it or not. I, personally,
have no problem with signing up kids for recreational sports to keep them active. But if your
daughter has been playing tennis for two years
and absolutely hates it, respect her feelings
when she tells you she doesn't want to play anymore.

If one of your kids seems to like a particular
sport, research local teams. Rec leagues abound,
and they're the ideal starting place for preschool
through elementary-school-aged children. Other parents will be able to tell you when kids are
eligible to try out for local competitive teams.
You'll have to decide if your son or daughter is
ready at that point. Keep in mind some competitive teams have virtually the same roster every
year—kids can't break into these teams unless
someone else drops out or is cut. In some cases,
the first year your child is able to try out will be
her best chance at getting on the team. Other
teams routinely weed out two or three kids a
year.

Sounds really unfair, doesn't it? Either your
child has to make the team the first year he tries
out or be on a team that routinely cuts players
deemed to be liabilities.

Sports, like life, aren't fair, and this won't change anytime soon.

Do Competitive Teams Really Matter?

You might be asking yourself what's the big deal? Why are parents so concerned with the type of team their kids play on?

Well...it's complicated.

I believe parents base decisions on a mixture of pride, worry, logic, and pragmatism in regards to youth sports.

We believe our children are as good as the other kids "moving up" to competitive teams. We worry that holding them back from tryouts could affect their ability to ever make the roster of a higher level team. Logic tells us their skills can only improve so much on their current rec league. Having knowledgeable coaches, more practice time, and playing against kids at the same or a higher level naturally increases our kids' skills. Pragmatically, we feel that it's wise for them to take a chance, to try out even if they don't make the cut.

There's also a perception that parents might as well kiss their kids' future dreams of high school sports goodbye if they aren't on travel teams as soon as they're of age. I have no concrete proof if this is true or not. I searched statistics but could not find any studies showing if there was a direct correlation between years of competing on competitive teams with playing varsity sports. My guess is the data doesn't exist because this is such a relatively new phenomenon.

The question of having your children play on competitive teams depends on a lot of factors. Is your school district full of kids who have access to competitive teams? What sports are popular in your district? How affluent is your community? What kind of state titles are big deals at the high school your kids will attend? How large or small is the high school?

If the majority of the kids in your community do not play on competitive teams, your children will likely develop similar skill sets as their peers without playing on them either. However, if you can't drive half a mile without seeing parents cheering at soccer fields, baseball diamonds, and tennis courts, you should at least consider the local teams that hold tryouts.

If your community is middle-class or upper-class, you're probably smack dab in the middle of competitive teams. It's not even a question.

In fact, your kids are probably already on travel teams.

If not, they certainly don't *have* to play on them. Good rec leagues will develop their talent, but if you're worried, there are other ways to build skills if you don't want to go the competitive team route. Private lessons, summer camps, and regular practice are valid options, too.

Consider the particulars of your school district's sports program. If the local high school took the state title for wrestling four of the previous six years, you can assume wrestling is a big deal in your area. If your son wants to wrestle, start him young. Ditto for any other sports.

As for the size of the high school, this could work out to your advantage or not. If you're in a small school district, there are fewer kids available to try out for sports. However, some small schools have an extremely talented pool of kids. Larger schools have more players trying out, but that doesn't necessarily mean all of them are talented. It really depends on your area.

From what I've observed, the perception that playing on competitive teams increases a kid's chance to play in high school is based on truth. Kids on competitive teams tend to have access to coaches who show them correct techniques.

They get years of quality practices, and they compete against teams at their level or higher. Simply put, they're all but guaranteed the practice and knowledge it takes to excel. Kids with natural talent who aren't on competitive teams have less playing time and limited access to experienced coaches. They may still make the team, but they are up against a very talented group of players.

The bottom line? More and more schools have access to highly trained athletes.

The cheerleading hopes of teens across America are shattered if they never took tumbling classes and can't do a back handspring. High school football players with natural talent but no experience will practice for hours with the team but will sit on the bench game after game. The kid who dominated in soccer on a recreation league makes the freshman soccer team but is cut the next year because the kids who played on travel teams have an edge.

All this puts tremendous pressure on kids and parents. Add dwindling school budgets and the increasing trend toward pay-to-play, and school sports are growing out of reach for many kids. Plenty of families can't afford travel teams and the expensive gear prevalent in these activities. Their kids are left behind, and the parents don't realize until it's too late. Worrying about how to come up with pay-to-play fees in high school won't help if your kid can't make the team to begin with.

High School And Varsity Sports

Do I really have to worry about high school and varsity sports when my kid is eight?

No.

Well...yes.

No, you don't have to worry. But here's why you will.

Your sweet little eight-year-old is singing to herself as she colors a picture at the kitchen table. You can barely imagine this third-grader going off to high school. She's still learning multiplication, for crying out loud! High school is eons away. Who cares if she plays a sport now? Or ever?

This is the right attitude. Eight is a blessed age. She still runs into your arms and hugs you regularly. Her problems can often be soothed with a kind word and a cookie. Her future looks as bright and lovely as her cute little face.

Fast forward four years to when she's twelve. She got braces last year, and she had a massive growth spurt over the summer. Her gangly legs, metal-bound teeth, and changing friendships bring out her insecurities. You assure her she's going to be okay, that she doesn't need to worry about her teeth or legs or friends. But last week one of the girls from school invited a bunch of your daughter's friends to a movie but didn't invite her. She's been moping ever since. Your heart hurts. No kind word from you or cookie will make it better.

You don't know how to help her through this time. Adolescence is tough. You hate this helpless feeling of wanting to make it all better but having no clue where to start.

The next day your daughter comes home ecstatic because one of her friends is trying out for a travel volleyball team. Your sweetheart is glowing with excitement as she claims it looks like fun and she wants to play on the same team.

You get excited because she's so thrilled. It will be nice for her to get some exercise and have another group of friends to spend time with.

You call the mom and learn her daughter has gone to volleyball summer camps two years in a row and played on a travel team the previous year.

Ouch. Your daughter has never touched a volleyball. You literally have no idea what gear is needed or what's even involved. The fees sound expensive. Also, you'll have to spend several weekends out of town in hotels for tournaments.

You try to push away the twinges of worry. Instead, you enjoy your daughter's enthusiasm, drive her to a sporting goods store, and buy kneepads, shorts, new athletic shoes, and, of course, a volleyball. You set up a net in the backyard and try to bounce the ball back and forth with her. Maybe her friend comes over a few afternoons to teach her basic moves.

The tryouts come around, and you take her to the gym. She's nervous but eager. You're relieved to see her outfit looks similar to what the other girls are wearing. You find a spot in the bleachers, and within minutes, it is crystal clear your daughter has no chance of making this team. The girls down there look like they've been playing since birth. Maybe even in the womb. Your daughter can't serve the ball over the net underhand let alone overhand.

When it's over, she's discouraged but still hopeful. She chews her fingernails to the quick until the calls are made, and she finds out she didn't make the team.

You swallow the lump in your throat. For three years in a row, your daughter has brought home a flyer for a local summer volleyball camp along with a stack of forms for other activities. You always gave them a cursory glance then tossed them in the trash. Now you wish you would have taken her to one of those camps.

You encourage your daughter to try out again next year. You offer to find a club for her to learn the basics. She refuses. She "doesn't really like volleyball" anyway.

Okay, so she doesn't like volleyball. What does she like?

This is when it hits you. Your daughter doesn't have much experience in *any* sport. Sure, she's athletic. She's taken a few swim lessons, played softball when she was little, spent a few years on a recreational soccer team. All her friends have been playing soccer, volleyball, basketball, tennis, and who knows what else for years. And your daughter?

Will most likely be cut from any high school sport that holds tryouts.

It's okay. She is still bright and beautiful. But your school district is sports crazy, and you missed the boat a few years ago when all her friends jumped on board. Maybe your daughter doesn't care. Maybe she'll be drawn to the art scene, the drama department, the robotics club, or the band. She'll be fine.

But if she does care, it will be difficult to play catch up to kids who've been developing their skills for years.

This scenario is extreme, but you get the point. Not all kids care about sports, but I'm guessing your children do or you wouldn't have picked up this book. I'm not trying to scare you. It's just a reality in communities all across America.

When your child tries out for a competitive team, be prepared. She'll probably be nervous. If she doesn't make the team, she might take it hard. If she truly likes the sport, encourage her to keep playing. If she makes the team, she's going to have a new set of issues to deal with like figuring out how she fits in with her teammates, wondering what position she'll play, fretting about if she'll get along with the coaches. This is normal, so don't worry if she's high strung for a while.

On the other hand, she might get cocky. After all, she made the team. This must mean she's elite—way better than the girls who didn't make it. Gently remind her that there are thousands of teams just like hers across America. She didn't qualify for the Olympics—she needs to bring the attitude down a notch. Prima-donnas are no fun to be around.

Whether your child is selected to be on a competitive team or not, remember you're going to be living in your community indefinitely. Treat the players and parents around you with respect. Don't rub it in if your kid makes a team when you know theirs didn't. Be respectful. You don't want to be embarrassed to look someone in the eye ten years from now.

Keep your eyes wide open to the reality of youth sports. Take advantage of local recreational teams when your kids are young. As they get older, talk to parents in your area about options such as competitive teams and summer camps. Many schools offer organized sports starting in seventh grade. Some have low-cost programs even earlier. If a competitive team appears to be the right choice, find out the fees and time commitments before tryouts are held. Check out other teams in your area—some are more budget friendly than others. Be prepared for team fees, equipment upgrades, out-of-town

tournament costs, possible fundraising requirements, and higher pressure for your children to
perform.

Yes, the world is more competitive. But we
can keep a level head about it.

Truths to Take Away:

1. Kids are training younger and specializing earlier.

2. Competitive teams (travel teams, all-star teams, tournament teams) are popping up everywhere and, depending on your community, may have become the new normal.

3. Kids can get the skills needed for higher level play in a number of ways. Competitive teams are not the only option. Local recreation leagues will get them playing time, and most urban areas offer specialized lessons specific to a sport. Check with your school district or local colleges about summer skills camps for kids.

4. Pray for guidance when unsure if your child should try out for a team or not.

CHAPTER SIX

But What About College Scholarships?

"Many are the plans in a person's heart, but it is the Lord's purpose that prevails." Proverbs 19:21 (NIV)

Johnny runs around in his team T-shirt with the rest of the four-year-olds signed up for soccer. It's his first organized sport, and he loves running, kicking the ball, and even taking a break while a parent hands out juice boxes and animal crackers.

Before you know it, Johnny is nine and still having fun playing soccer with his friends. He's also getting better. There are several standouts on the team, and he's one of them. At the end of the season, a few parents mention the travel team their boys are trying out for in the spring. You talk it over with Johnny, and he decides he wants to try out, too. He makes the roster, and so begins his time playing on competitive teams.

Each year brings more equipment to buy, more travel expenses, more stress, and more scheduling conflicts, but Johnny is becoming a good player. Yes, he has his ups and downs. The positions aren't always fair, and last season he wasn't as aggressive as a few of the other kids. Some practices he couldn't wait for, and others he had to be dragged to.

At times you wonder if it's still in his best interests to play. Even if you occasionally fantasize about having him skip tryouts for the travel team next year, you squash the thought. If Johnny wants to play in high school, he needs to be able to compete at the same level as his peers. Both the junior varsity and varsity high school teams are known for being tough. And who knows? He could get a college scholarship out of it.

Hold it right there.

These two words make me cringe: college scholarship. They didn't always bother me, but in recent years they do. I believe parents use this goal as an excuse for taking competitiveness to the extreme.

The Truth About Athletic Scholarships

Athletic college scholarships. The holy grail of many parents with kids in competitive sports. I confess I knew next to nothing about them until I began researching the topic for this book. I assumed a varsity letter combined with talent gave a high school athlete a good shot at getting a scholarship. Well, I was wrong.

I did a little research and found some eye-opening statistics. First, let's look at the chances of a high school kid even playing in college. The article "Odds of a High School Athlete Playing College Sports" from www.scholarshipstats.com,[4] shares statistics for all high school sports based on U.S. high schools and U.S. colleges (2013-2014).

Take two popular boys' sports, football and basketball. The total number of men playing football in college compared to the number of boys playing in high school is 8.0%. This means 92% of high school football players will NOT play in college.

The total number of men playing basketball in college compared to the number of boys playing in high school is 5.9%. This means 94.1% of male high school basketball players will NOT play in college.

Now let's look at two popular girls' sports, softball and volleyball. The total number of women playing softball in college compared to the number of girls playing in high school is 8.3%. This means that 91.7% of high school softball players will NOT play in college.

The total number of women playing volleyball in college compared to the number of girls playing in high school is 6.2%. This means that 93.8% of high school volleyball players will NOT play in college.

Check out the complete list in the article above, and you'll see the numbers are similar for all sports. There are several exceptions, like fencing (both boys and girls), but most kids playing a high school sport have less than a 1 in 10 chance of playing in college.

And what about those scholarships we discussed?

The above study *only* takes participation into account. This does not mean the students playing sports in college are awarded any financial scholarships.

In "Chances of a High School Athlete Getting an Athletic Scholarship" also from www.scholarshipstats.com,[5] the number of high school players are compared to the number of available scholarships for that sport (2013-2014).

Let's look at football and basketball again. There are forty-three high school football players for every athletic scholarship available, and only one in three college football players is awarded a scholarship. There are fifty-seven high school boy basketball players per one athletic scholarship, and there are 2.3 college players per one scholarship available.

What about softball and volleyball? For every fifty high school girls playing softball, there is one athletic scholarship available, and for every three women playing softball in college, only one has an athletic scholarship. There are fifty-three high school girl volleyball players per one athletic scholarship, and 2.5 college players per one scholarship available.

According to "Athletic Scholarships for College Students" from www.debt.org,[6] athletic scholarships are awarded to less than 2% of undergraduate students in the United States. For all sports, the average athletic scholarship amounts to approximately $9,000, and according to NCAA rules, no scholarship is guaranteed for a full four years.

No guarantee? No problem. Right?

Wrong.

Even if your son or daughter is an elite athlete and earns a scholarship, it might only cover a portion of tuition or be awarded for just one year. To be accepted into the university, your child will need to meet or exceed the NCAA requirements which increased as of 2016. NCAA D1 schools have stricter conditions than NCAA D2 schools. For the list of minimum GPA and core course requirements, refer to "Make Sure You Meet the NCAA and NAIA College Academic Requirements" at www.athleticscholarships.net.[7] Even if your student meets the minimum conditions, she's not assured to be accepted into the school. Keep in mind, she'll be expected to maintain amateur status as well as a certain grade point average, and she'll need to complete a minimum amount of credit hours each quarter or semester to remain eligible at the college she attends.

Other Realities Of College Sports

Say your daughter is awarded an athletic scholarship and moves out of state to play volleyball for a well-known public university. The scholarship covers the cost of her tuition, but it doesn't include her room and board or her out-of-state fees. Even with the "full ride" of tuition, over the course of four years she will owe between $40,000 and $200,000, depending on the university. How will she afford this?

The "full ride" doesn't look as *full* as we'd hoped.

We gloss over the harsh realities of sports until they glare at us.

What do we really want for our babies? Bragging rights? A lifetime of debt?

Additionally, recent studies found a disturbing trend among college athletes experiencing depression or overwhelming anxiety. The 2014 article from www.NCAA.org, "Mind, Body and Sport: Depression and Anxiety Prevalence in Student Athletes,"[8] looked at a variety of depression and anxiety indicators for all college students, and they found that student athletes are less likely than their non-athlete peers to seek help with anxiety or depression. These mental conditions affect their performance on the field and in the classroom. If left untreated, student athletes dealing with anxiety or depression might turn to risky behaviors. High levels of stress in the previous twelve months was one of the highest predictors of depression and anxiety. Let's face it, stress and athletic performance go hand-in-hand.

The stakes are high for college athletic departments to produce winning teams, and this puts additional stress on student athletes. Players have to miss classes to travel for games. Practices and training take many hours each week. Schedule conflicts, demands on their time, and the pressure of competition are all factors contributing to anxiety.

I'm not discouraging your son or daughter from signing with a university to play the sport they love. But if they're asked to play without a scholarship, I hope they'll weigh their options and make the best decision for their future. Sometimes playing for an in-state or local college will be a better choice than an out-of-state university. They will be closer to home, more likely to see friends and family, and the costs are usually lower.

You might be thinking that this book isn't about college sports. We're just a bunch of parents trying to help our kids through youth sports.

Go back to chapter one and review the reasons why you want your kid to play sports. If one of your answers includes earning a college scholarship, you might want to demote it to the bottom of the list. I'm not saying she won't get a scholarship. I am saying don't count on it.

Some of you are shaking your head right now. *Why in the world is a high school spot or college scholarship the goal for your children?* I don't blame you. For many parents and kids, these are valid aspirations. But for the vast majority of kids who do not play in high school or college? They grow up to be successful people.

Instead of buying into society's idea of why kids play youth sports, define your own. Keep it close to you. Yes, you'll lose sight of it on occasion, but go back to it often. If you don't, you could get caught in the trap of pushing your kids to earn a college scholarship that might not be in their best interests.

Truths to Take Away:

1. Less than 10% of all high school athletes in the United States will participate in college sports.

2. Of those 10%, only 2% will be awarded any form of athletic scholarship.

3. Scholarships are not guaranteed for all four years of undergraduate studies.

4. Out-of-state tuition is usually more expensive than in-state tuition.

5. The reason kids play sports is different for each family, but a varsity letter and/or college scholarship should only be a small part of the answer.

CHAPTER SEVEN

Politics And Dynamics Of Team Parents

*"Be still before the Lord and wait patiently for him;
do not fret when people succeed in their ways,
when they carry out their wicked ways." Psalm
37:7 (NIV)*

If you're new to youth sports, you might not know this, but kids aren't the only ones who get a team—parents get one, too. Good or bad, you're part of a tribe—the parent tribe. Some sports require minimal parental involvement while others are more intense with parents sitting together for entire weekends to cheer on their kids.

No matter what types of teams your kids join, you will hopefully find some incredibly nice parents. You also might find some members of your new tribe who are hard core, negative, or just plain rude. That's okay. You don't have to be best buddies with them. Hey, you don't even have to sit next to them.

Parent Tribes

These parent tribes are important. They can make your life easier. I regularly work with other parents to carpool and to verify I'm looking at the schedule correctly. I enjoy cheering with them, and I'm blessed to call many of them friends.

Tribes can be difficult, too. For one thing, they're always changing. Each season brings a shift. Players come and go, as do their parents. If your child switches teams, you must assimilate with a new tribe.

Parents—myself included—can unintentionally slight other members of the tribe. We forget to introduce ourselves to the newcomers, act standoffish during games, or only talk to our close friends. The system is not set up well. Our kids are jockeying for playing time, positions, and coaching favor, yet we parents are supposed to get along.

The result? Sometimes the tribe behaves; sometimes it doesn't.

Before you pick your spot on the bleachers, set up your chair near the sidelines, or attend the introductory parent meeting, understand what you'll likely face during the season.

1. Parents "coaching" their kids from the sidelines.
2. Parents complaining about the team, the coaches, other players, their own kid, you name it.
3. Parents cheering, sometimes loudly.
4. Parents being rude to another parent during a game.
5. Parents embarrassed when grandparents witness a bad play or loss.
6. Groups of parents who are close friends who make others feel left out.
7. Parents off by themselves.
8. Siblings. Of all ages. Everywhere.

We don't have any control over other parents' behavior, but we certainly can control ours. We choose how to treat the members of our tribe.

Maybe we're not always in a chatty mood, but for the most part, we can make an effort to greet all team parents, not just the ones we're friends with. If sitting next to the perpetually negative parent puts us in a murderous mood, we can make a conscious effort to sit next to a parent who doesn't raise our hackles.

Most of all, we can do our best to encourage the other moms and dads by supporting their children. Cheer for every player. Try not to feed off of anyone's competitiveness—just give them as much grace as you can muster.

How do we handle the complaining parent? Well, we're not perfect. I certainly do my share of complaining no matter how hard I try not to. Most of us have times when we're insecure about our kid's performance. If a parent who normally doesn't complain starts griping, just listen. Sometimes we simply need a kind shoulder to lean on and a little reassurance.

What about the perpetual complainer? The parent who thinks the coach is terrible and every player is worthless—except for *his kid*, of course—the one who never has a nice thing to say?

Again, grace. Be nice. Be friendly, but remember there is no rule that says you have to be friends with this person. Avoid them if they're getting on your nerves.

Sometimes you're stuck with extremely difficult tribe members. The parent who heckles players *on your own team*? The one yelling at their kid constantly? The other who gets on the phone with the coach to bad mouth *your* child while casually mentioning *hers* is better equipped for the position?

I'm shaking my head. We've experienced this. It's hard. I wish I could say you won't turn into a flaming ball of rage—but I can't guarantee that. I know I've had sleepless nights over parent injustices.

How do we handle this? I don't have the answer. I can only say my husband and I have done our best to not retaliate or respond to this type of negativity. These are unhappy people who are clearly living vicariously through their children. If someone is heckling other players on your team, you have every right to confront them—peacefully—about it. Try not to add to the tension. Simply ask them to respect the players. This might not work, but at least you did something. Also, tell your kid that you condemn any behavior that doesn't support the team.

Hopefully, these types of scenarios are rare or nonexistent within your tribe.

The Outsider Syndrome

At some point in your child's sports career, you might have to move, or your kid switches teams or tries a new sport. When you move to a new town, you typically don't know anyone, so you dig a little and find out when tryouts are held for the sport your child wants to play. At the tryout date, adults are chatting with each other. They clearly know the other parents, kids, and coaches. No one knows you or your child. You worry that being unknown will cost your kid a spot on the team.

Sometimes it does. Some teams are virtually impossible to break into. The coaches chose a roster when the kids were young, nurtured them, and continue to put their trust in the original team for as long as every player wants to play. But as kids grow, they change. Some decide to concentrate on a different sport, or they quit altogether. Others are physically unable to keep up with the rest of the team.

Let's say that after the tryouts, you get the call that your kid made the cut. If this is an established team, you are now the new member of an existing tribe. You're an outsider. And so is your child.

The outsider syndrome can be good and bad. Coaches already know the strengths and weaknesses of their existing players, so they may pay extra attention to your child. However, if your kid fails to live up to their expectations, they may put more emphasis on his weaknesses and less on his strengths. This can lead to decreased playing time or being kept from playing a position he's qualified for.

Other parents might feel threatened by your child's presence, especially if he is being groomed for the position their child usually plays. This might result in them watching for him to make a mistake and using this information against him. Since you're outsiders, the coaches don't really know you or your son and are less likely to give you the benefit of the doubt.

Also, there can be unforeseen consequences if your kid plays a school-sponsored sport but doesn't attend the school in question (she goes to a private school or is homeschooled). Other parents might use this information to try to get a better position for their child. After all, your daughter doesn't even go to that school. Your daughter might feel left out. The other girls all banter with each other, and since they're secure that they're "one of the team" they might not even think to include her. This can lead to her not enjoying the sport as much as she should because she doesn't feel like she belongs.

She's not accepted, and it hurts her not only emotionally, but on the field, too. Team sports require multiple players working together. If your daughter isn't accepted as a valued member of the team, she will not have the trust of the other players. In games, they'll rely on their friends more than on her.

We can help our children through this outsider phase. When we make an effort with other parents, those parents get to know us. And when they get to know us—and hopefully like us—they have a positive feeling about our kids. They might cheer for them more, and this attitude trickles down to their kids. Before long our kids are laughing with other players and have become accepted members of the team.

If you're an outsider, try to get other parents' contact information. This will help with carpooling or if you get lost on the way to a tournament and need directions. Chat with other parents at practices and games. Make an effort, even when it feels uncomfortable.

Try to get along with parents for your children's sake because one thing you won't be able to protect your babies from? Politics.

Politics + Sports = A Nightmare

Oh, how I wish politics didn't exist in sports! Unfortunately, youth sports are a petri dish teeming with political schemes by parents, coaches, and other players. My husband and I work hard to refrain from engaging in politics. We push aside our doubts and trust God to work things out for our kids, but it's not easy. And as children grow older, advancing to higher skill levels, the politics get worse.

Let's start at the most obvious and prevalent area where politics exist—at the top.

The coach.

I'm deeply grateful for coaches of youth sports. They give up huge chunks of their time to develop players and mold a team. They rarely get paid. They have good intentions. They are doing this to help the next generation of kids not only enjoy sports, but also to become better players.

That being said, the majority of youth sports teams across America have parent coaches. This means that the coach has a child on the team.

How do politics play into the parent-coach situation?

- Either the coach's kid gets one of the best positions or, in a misguided attempt to be fair, one of the worst.
- The coach may be friends with several parents on the team. This puts her in an awkward situation. The friends might campaign for better positions for their kids. They also might withhold their friendship at any perceived injustice.
- Coaches are under tremendous pressure to win. If they are coaching competitive sports, they may need to convince strong players to try out for the team. This could put them in an ethical dilemma. Do they promise a position to a new player, which means bumping an existing valuable player to a lesser spot? It's not fair to the current player, but coaches sometimes do this to put together a winning team. Some parents demand guarantees—maybe a certain position or playing time—before committing their child.

Then we come to the parents. I'm dumbfounded at the lengths parents will go to get what they want for their kid.

Some ways parents play politics:

- Parents offer to be assistant coaches solely to get their child a coveted position.
- Parents help out with practices, tipping favor to their child.

- Parents calling the coach to complain about other players, exalt their own kid, or to get more playing time.
- Parents rallying to have a coach removed because the coach didn't do what they wanted.
- Parents pushing their child to be best friends with a star player to be associated with being the best.
- Parents promising money for fundraising or sponsoring the team to influence whether their kid makes the roster or not.
- Parents forming cliques or alliances with other parents to further their child's chances of staying on the team next season.

The way teams are constructed is based on more than the players' abilities. The most deserving kids don't always get the best positions or the same amount of playing time as less talented players. All because of politics.

I'd love to know the answers on how to handle these situations, but I muddle my way through the best I can. There are some things you can't do much about. Coaches tend to favor their children. They also may be swayed by scheming parents to limit your kid's playing time in order to give the other parents' child more. You can talk to the coach, but you probably will just hear justifications on why you're wrong and he's right.

We tell our kids to give each practice and game one hundred percent whether they're being treated fairly or not. We recognize the politics around us, and we realize every team has them to some degree. Usually our children are playing locally with kids they get along with. I can overlook a lot of politics if practices and games are conveniently located and my kids are playing with friends. But if the situation becomes too difficult, consider having your child try out for a different team the following season.

If scheming works, why not join the other parents playing politics?

I don't recommend it.

Remember, once you start "playing the game," you become embroiled in a competitive battle with other parents. You're on a slippery slope to getting a distorted view of the team. Adults who play these games tend to overlook their kids' weaknesses and focus on finding faults in their teammates. That's depressing. When we can no longer be objective about children who are playing a game, we need to give ourselves a time out. Think hard before calling the coach to complain about another player. Is this really what you want your kids to learn?

That backstabbing a teammate is the way to get ahead?

Try not to be afraid when other people's schemes work. Just remember why your kids are playing in the first place.

We can't avoid politics altogether, but we can choose not to rely on them to get our way. Let your kids earn their spots on teams, and when they make it, support them without playing the political game.

Truths to Take Away:

1. Good or bad, parents are together during their kids' sports seasons. We can be positive influences or negative ones.

2. New players to an existing team are outsiders, and this can affect their performance. Encourage the team to welcome the new kids.

3. Some parents don't want your child to succeed because they believe it threatens their kid's position. They *will* play politics which negatively affect your child. Choose not to engage in this behavior. It only sends the wrong message to your kid.

CHAPTER EIGHT

What Your Kid Needs From You

"Follow God's example, therefore, as dearly loved children and walk in the way of love, just as Christ loved us and gave himself up for us as a fragrant offering and sacrifice to God." Ephesians 5:1-2 (NIV)

Your daughter kicks the winning goal into the soccer net. The sidelines explode! She did it! The proud moment lingers as the team convenes at a local ice cream shop. Everyone is in a good mood—well, it seems that way to you. But hiding behind the smiling parents and teammates, all is not well. One mother seethes. Her daughter kicked an opponent in the ankle and, rather than getting a warning, she was pulled from the game earlier.

Can't the kid make one measly mistake? Another parent can't believe the coach didn't play his little girl at all. *Why couldn't my daughter have made that shot? If she would just get a chance to play, she'd be the hero for once.*

When our children are competing, sports can be rough on our egos. Feelings bombard us. Sometimes we handle these complicated emotions well. Sometimes our inner two-year-olds override the mature parts of our brain, and too often, we model behavior that is the direct opposite of how we want our kids to act.

Modeling Poor Behavior

We aren't being positive role models when we're:

- Publicly complaining to coaches
- Yelling at refs for perceived bad calls
- Bad-mouthing teammates in front of our children
- Acting like drill sergeants during practices or at games
- Coaching our kids from the bleachers
- Coaching other players from the bleachers
- Putting unrealistic expectations on young players
- Arguing with a coach or parent in public

It's normal to want to help our kids succeed. We're used to anticipating their needs. It's why we packed diaper bags when they were babies. Sports are just another area where we want to provide guidance.

This guidance is often misguided.

Let's break down the above list.

There is a time and place for parents to have a discussion with the coach about something bothering them. In front of an audience is not the time or the place. If you truly can't live another day without addressing the issue, contact the coach privately. Continuously complaining (even if you feel down to your bone marrow your complaint is justified) is counterproductive. It gives the coach the impression you do not respect him. We should be encouraging our kids to respect people in authority. Notice I said respect, not blindly agree with everything.

You will experience a time when you strongly disagree with a coach's decision. It's inevitable. Hopefully, you've taken the steps mentioned in the earlier chapters and defined why you have your kids playing sports. When you're freaking out, take a step back. Ask yourself how this issue will affect your child in ten years. If your blood pressure is still at molten lava levels, look even further, thirty years. Will this season really matter in the long run? I don't think so.

But maybe you're convinced it will. Maybe you have dreams of Susie playing in high school and college. Well, varsity coaches don't put up with parent interference, and college coaches expect players to compete for their spots. Use this knowledge to prepare yourself—and your child—for future greatness. How many kids head off to college with a chip on their shoulder because they were superstars in their hometown? Suddenly they're surrounded by kids just as, if not more, talented than they are. Can Mom or Dad call the coach and complain about their playing time? Not without getting laughed at or worse.

The next item on the list involves yelling at referees/umpires. It's one thing to sit on the bleachers and complain about a questionable decision. It's another to get in referees' faces and scream at them. They're human. They make bad calls sometimes. Can we adults show our kids that a bad call or two will not ruin their entire life? These officials could be at home having fun with their families. Most are not paid big bucks. They do it because they love the game.

Then there's bad-mouthing a teammate in front of your children. This is never a good idea. Remember, these kids are just that—kids. They aren't perfect. Yeah, some have bad attitudes or show less energy than we think they should—but they are on the team. Our family rule? Always support every member of your team. That means our children have to cheer for their teammates, show grace at others' mistakes, and brush off any rude comments from difficult players. We adults do, too. Not easily done by any of us.

What about acting like drill sergeants? Have you ever yelled out tips to your kids during practices or at games? I have. But it's the last thing our kids need! That's why they have coaches. Parents need to step *waaay* back on this one. Our kids know how to play. If they don't, the coach will not hesitate to tell them. But we're so controlling, we never miss an opportunity to "help" our children. At the best, when we yell tips to them, we're a distraction. At the worst, we're making it clear to everyone around us that our kids *do not know what they're doing.* Let's not embarrass them. Trust them. They will make mistakes. They won't always have proper form. Yelling tips will not change this. If you want to help, do it at home, not in front of everyone. Think about it. When you go to work, do you need your boss stopping by and telling you how to do your job every five minutes? Maybe your boss thinks she's helping, but it doesn't come across that way. All you can think is, *let me do my job, lady. I'm not a moron!*

Seasoned players don't need our tips. They need to be allowed to practice, play, and make mistakes. The only thing our kids really want from us is genuine support. They want us to be there for them. They want us to enjoy their sports, and we should be able to tell them we like watching them play.

What about "helping" other players on the team by coaching them from the sidelines? No. Just no. Not during a game. Not during a practice. Not ever, unless the child, the parents, or the coaches ask you to help.

Moving on... How do you know if you're putting unrealistic expectations on young players? If you expect them to be perfect every time they compete, you have unrealistic expectations. If any mistake makes you cringe, you need to check your attitude. Kids are developing, they're physically, mentally, and emotionally immature, and that's okay.

The final item on the list is arguing with a parent or coach in public. Tempers flare during sports—I get it. But public verbal brawls aren't good for anyone. It's not the message we should be sending. If we have a problem with parents or a coach, we need to contact them privately about it.

Modeling Good Behavior

Guess what? While parents are busy creating a high-stakes atmosphere and making sports more of a job than an extracurricular activity, the kids on the field, in the pool, on the ice, and in the gym are actually having fun.

Fun! Yes! What a crazy concept.

Your child should be playing the sport because she enjoys it. And if she likes it, shouldn't you enjoy watching her?

Of course, sports won't be fun every day. There are times when they're no fun. Hopefully, though, the good days outnumber the bad.

Please take a minute to think about your children playing their favorite sports. Does it bring a smile to your face? If it doesn't, why not? Can you think of times when they just seemed full of joy playing? Hang onto that.

That's the good stuff—that's why they're out there.

Instead of focusing on their deficiencies, we should be searching for their strengths.

Our kids desperately need to know we approve of them.

We get so busy parenting we forget our kids look up to us. We're their heroes. They might not always obey us, but their ears pick up our words, and their eyes watch our actions. Many of the things they do are motivated by their desire to get our attention. They want to impress us, and they yearn for unconditional love.

Don't we all?

I'm a grown woman, and I still long for parental approval and unconditional love. I know where to find it, too. Ephesians 5:1-2 sums up my feelings on being a child of God as well as a parent. "Follow God's example, therefore, as dearly loved children and walk in the way of love, just as Christ loved us and gave himself up for us as a fragrant offering and sacrifice to God."

We are dearly loved children. So dearly loved that God sent His Son to die for us to save us from our sins so that we can live with Him eternally in heaven. If God can love us that much, surely we can smile watching our kids play sports.

If we're always pointing out ways to improve our kids' skills, always fretting about playing time or position, always screaming from the sidelines instead of enjoying the game, our children will not feel we approve of them. They will correctly assume they need to *be better* to win our approval.

Our kids shouldn't have to perform well for us to approve of them. They should automatically have our approval simply for being our children.

How can we show our kids we approve of them? Sometimes it will mean telling them they had a great game. Other times it will mean not mentioning a mistake or ignoring their bad mood. There will be moments we'll have to discipline them to nip bad behavior in the bud. Even so, I hope we can always genuinely tell them we enjoy watching them play.

Someday, we'll reflect back on these days of running our children to practices, sitting through tough games, biting our nails, bristling over politics, washing uniforms, driving across town for a scrimmage, and high-fiving after a win, and we'll smile. I hope we cherish each moment we bonded with our kids as they played sports.

At the end of the day, it *is* just a game. Tomorrow comes, and the next day after that, and five years have gone by like a flash of lightning. Kids have many layers of life. School, friends, hobbies, vacations—there's much more to your children than the sports they play. This isn't their job. They have their entire lives to work, so encourage them to enjoy playing.

I hope our children's memories of sports include us supporting them, the bonding they shared playing as a team, and the lessons they learned from their coaches. But mostly, I hope they remember the fun. I hope we parents remember the fun, too.

Truths to Take Away:

1. Model the behavior you want your children to emulate.

2. It's just a sport, just a game. Sometimes it feels like the cusp of doom, but it's not. Let's not treat each game as though our life depends on it.

3. Kids should enjoy playing sports. It's why they're playing. If they aren't having fun, take a hard look at yourself as a parent and ask if you're contributing to that.

4. What do you want your children to remember about sports? That you were supportive? Or that you made them feel as if they could never live up to your expectations?

CHAPTER NINE

Avoid Bitterness; Embrace Joy

"But the fruit of the Spirit is love, joy, peace, forbearance, kindness, goodness, faithfulness, gentleness and self-control. Against such things there is no law." Galatians 5:22-23 (NIV)

W e've been talking about what our kids need, but I'll be honest, sometimes it's really hard to model good behavior, support them without making them feel inferior, *and* generally keep my act together. This chapter, my friends, is for me.

Yep. Me.

I had a season where I was a bitter hag. I could barely sleep. I was angry at the world—well, my little sports world—and I knew it was unhealthy, but I couldn't get over it. Probably because I was still in it. Every time I drove my kid to practice I'd hope the circumstances would change. I'd grit my teeth through games. Parents who I'd talked to and joked with mere weeks before annoyed me. Nothing pleased me, and nothing could please me.

Why?

My kid was in the middle of an unfair season full of petty politics, and there was nothing I could do about it. So I pouted and raged and didn't even pretend to smile through the pain. I'm not proud of this, but I had a hard time even looking at a few people.

I would love to tell you I'm overstating my feelings, but I was a mess, and I knew it.

I remember lying in bed at night as bitterness chewed at me. I couldn't sleep. I tried praying for the people responsible for the unfairness, but even my prayers felt insincere. The season never improved—we knew it wouldn't due to the politics—but, finally, it ended.

A few months later, I looked back and felt the rage all over again. I wondered why the situation still had power over me. Why couldn't I just shake it off and move on? I mean, I hadn't even been able to truly pray (and I mean pray in a good way) for those people. How sad is that?

I took some time to get on my knees and truly forgive the people who had wronged my child. I let go of the hate. A bitter taste lingered, though.

The experience changed me, but not overnight. In fact, I still have to consciously rise above my base emotions when sports aren't fair. Bitterness and anger are always simmering below the surface, ready to pounce where my kids are concerned. I try hard not to give in to those feelings. Sure, I have my moments when they sneak out, but I can't live like that—I won't live like that—ever again.

I've mentioned many situations that parents stew over. Unequal playing time. Favoritism. Losing a coveted position. Getting benched. Deserving to play on a competitive team but not making it when someone with less talent does. I could go on and on.

We can't prevent these things from happening. They occur every day, in every sport. Our kids will not always be treated fairly, especially when it comes to competitive sports. That doesn't mean we have to try to fix the situation.

We don't have to hate the people responsible. Nor should we lose sleep and grow bitter.

It's important to take a hard, honest look at why we're feeling the rage. It's easy to spout off all the she-did-me-wrong reasons to be so upset, but doing so only reinforces our feelings of helplessness and pushes us deeper into the ugly feelings.

Did I Fail My Child?

When I look back on that awful season, I believe I was bitter and angry because at some level I felt like I'd failed my child. Who enjoys feeling like a failure? I certainly don't. Instead of going inward and admitting this, I blamed everyone involved.

I'd naively believed my family wouldn't be affected by other parents' schemes, and I was wrong. My child's talent wasn't the issue. A combination of other things were. I felt helpless, like I should have prevented the situation.

And the reality? I didn't fail my child. I wish I could have recognized those feelings instead of focusing on the externals. It was a tough experience, but my kid survived. And grew stronger.

Another factor of my bitterness? The feeling my child was being left behind. You might think

I'm ridiculous, and I'll fully agree, but I worried an unfair season at such an early age would permanently damage my child's ego. Kids don't understand politics when they are young. They internalize, assume they're to blame for their reduced circumstances, when the truth is the opposite.

We worry that the mental stress of an injustice will cause our children not to take risks as they get older and to basically accept a mediocre life because they've been so burned in the past. I believe that's a major reason why parents interfere with coaches and get too involved in general. We don't want our kids crushed beyond repair.

We subconsciously worry any setback in a sport will cause a permanent setback in life.

The reality is quite different, though. Setbacks are opportunities to grow. Parents can help children by allowing them to push through tough seasons. We can talk to them about what is happening and ask them questions like in the following scenario.

"Why do you think you're no longer a soloist on the dance team?"

She shrugs. "I'm not good enough."

"You took second place at the last competition. You're good enough."

She ducks her chin. "My dance teacher doesn't like me."

"She likes you. Sometimes things happen that we can't control. When they do, we *can* control our reaction. Keep doing your best in class. You'll be ready if the teacher decides to give you a solo again."

This conversation doesn't blame anyone but it allows your daughter permission to move forward doing something she enjoys even when she's discouraged. If parent politics are blatantly obvious, you might want to have an honest conversation with her about it. It's your call.

Looking back on my bitter season, I wish I would have relied on my faith. On the truth in God's word. Psalm 37:7 encourages us to wait on the Lord. "Be still before the Lord and wait patiently for Him; do not fret when people succeed in their ways, when they carry out their wicked schemes." Romans 8:28 tells us that God is in control. "And we know that in all things God works for the good of those who love him, who have been called according to his purpose." I'm not saying unethical politics are God's will—

sin is never endorsed by God—but Scripture says He uses all things for His children's good.

We also feel helpless when we see some kids breeze through their sports' lives without all the obstacles our kids face. Sounds good, doesn't it? Wouldn't it be nice if our kids could breeze through, too?

Not really. Sure, it seems good. But when they get to higher levels of sports, they face real competition. The parents scheming to get them the position they want can only take their kids so far. At some point these players have to back it up by proving themselves on the field. If the coach at the next level doesn't like them? Their parents have no sway this time.

The players who have faced adversity and kept improving are the ones who develop the grit to play at higher levels. The stars with all the playing time who have never been benched? Aren't so sure of themselves when they're surrounded by athletes more talented than they are. Some buckle down and prove their worth. Others get chips on their shoulders, grandiose ideas about what they deserve. Ultimately, they end up disenchanted because life doesn't turn out the way they've been told it would their entire lives.

When our kids are young, we don't keep this overall view in mind. We ignore the facts. We see certain kids protected from the negative side of sports, and we internally, maybe subconsciously, try to position our kids to be protected, too. It's *why* we scream at refs after bad calls, contact the coach the instant we sense an inequity against our child, act like drill sergeants on the bleachers, and pour so much time and money into these extracurricular activities.

We're not only telling the world our kids are good enough, we're proclaiming that we are too.

All of this goes back to the lie.

When our kid gets treated unfairly, we burn with bitterness.

Their success isn't our success. Their failure isn't our failure. But their injustice sure feels like our injustice.

Resilience

Let's take a minute to look back. Go down memory lane and think back to when you were ten or thirteen or however old your child is currently. Were you playing a sport? Were you good at it? How did the coach treat you? How did your teammates treat you? Were you a star player? If not, who was?

Do you remember any setbacks? Any moments that bring a flush of shame even now?

What about the big moments—what happened that made you feel great?

The only activity I cared about as a kid was dance. In junior high, I played soccer, was a cheerleader, and competed in track. Additionally, from third to eighth grade I played basketball, but I wasn't very good. My parents made me play. I had many, many bad moments in basketball. Offense, defense—it didn't matter—the whole sport scared me, and I wanted nothing more than to sit on the bench every game. I actually hyperventilated when I was in eighth grade because I almost fouled out. Boy, my mom was embarrassed about that! Here's the thing, though. Basketball didn't affect my ego or confidence even though I was terrible at it. Why? I never wanted to play in the first place. I intrinsically knew it wasn't my thing, but my parents thought it would be good for me. And honestly, playing the sport did me no long-term harm.

When you're not emotionally invested in something—when it isn't fun for you on any level—you don't get scarred from it.

Dance, on the other hand, was embedded in my soul. I'd begged for and took a few tumbling and jazz classes over the years, and in high school I tried out for the pompon team, otherwise known as the dance team. I gave tryouts everything I had and held my breath until I found out I had made it.

Since I was so emotionally invested in this activity, any setback felt catastrophic. I worked harder and harder to learn the routines and to be the best I could be. There were better dancers than me on the team, but I never felt inferior because I knew in my heart I was giving it my all.

I believed in myself and my abilities. I loved being on the team. Setbacks happened, and I met them head-on by trying even harder.

If your child is in a competitive sport, I'm guessing he loves it and is good at it. He probably believes in his abilities. He wants to be on the team (most of the time, anyway). You can safely assume he will have setbacks, and I urge you to trust that he will work hard to overcome them. He might be in a situation where no matter how hard he works, he will not get ahead. I hope you encourage him to continue to give every practice and game one hundred percent. We gain self-confidence when we work hard without any guarantees our effort will pay off.

Sometimes the sweetest victories are the ones no one applauds.

It's shooting ten free throws in a row at practice for the first time. The first overhand serve that makes it over the net. Running suicides without wanting to puke. Doing a handstand on the balance beam. Striking out a batter with a full pitch count. Meeting the weight goal for wrestling. Getting the rebound and scoring the goal into the hockey net.

Confidence develops from improving our skills and overcoming setbacks. It can be nourished by parents and coaches, but ultimately, it's an individual's hard work at something that makes them believe in their abilities. No matter how many times you tell someone they are good at something, it isn't until they accept it deep within themselves that their confidence develops.

As much as we want to protect our kids from pain, the tough times are opportunities for our kids to grow.

So how can we take all of this information and use it to avoid bitterness and embrace joy?

Avoid Bitterness

If you're in the middle of an unfair situation concerning sports, my condolences. Like I said, I've been there.

First, know you aren't alone. With all the millions of kids in sports and the abundance of stories about parents behaving badly at games, it's safe to say that there are many parents who are mired in bitterness as we speak. Focusing on all the reasons your kid's situation is unfair will not change anything. Being angry and full of hate won't either.

Here are my suggestions.

1. Articulate what your child is going through. Mentally list all the things that are bothering you about the situation. Write them down if necessary.

2. Review the list. What is the worst that can happen if the situation doesn't improve? (Feel free to go down worst-case-scenario road. *Johnny will lose all faith in the good of mankind, get addicted to crystal meth, and end up in jail or dead.* Hey, I'm melodramatic. I can come up with some doozies for outcomes.)

3. Is my worst case scenario realistic? Does it reflect my child's true personality, or

is it just a big blob of my fears? We don't always give our kids credit to bounce back from tough times. They're more resilient than we think.

4. How can I help my child grow from this? Remember, struggles are opportunities for us to become stronger. Hopefully, your answers include things along the lines of, she'll learn that hard work is its own reward, or she'll believe in herself when no one else does. If we want our kids to grow up to be successful, moral adults, we can encourage them to handle setbacks and unfairness with dignity.

5. Are my words and actions promoting a victim mentality in myself or my kid?

6. Remind yourself why you have your kids play sports. Chances are you'll see this as an opportunity for them to grow.

7. If you're angry at a coach or parent, do your best to view them objectively. They have reasons for acting the way they do. You don't have to like these people, but you don't have to hate them, either.

8. Talk with your child about what is happening. Kids blame themselves for everything. If she's convinced the coach

doesn't like her or that she's not very good, explain to her there could be other reasons she's not playing as much. Tell her to keep working hard. If we want our kids to grow in confidence, we need to help them emotionally and mentally navigate these injustices instead of allowing them to internalize false beliefs.

9. Whenever you feel the prickly-can't-breathe bitter feeling, practice stress relief. Take deep breaths. Find your mental peaceful place. Remind yourself this too shall pass. Review the affirmations and Bible passages listed in Chapter Thirteen. These free lists are on my website, jillkemerer.com/books/game-on/, in pdf form to download, print or copy/paste to your phone.

10. Recognize the warning signs that you're getting upset. If you're at a game or practice and worried you're going to start acting inappropriately, walk away for a few minutes. If that isn't possible, take deep breaths. Although it's difficult, we can control ourselves.

11. Consider journaling. I find writing my thoughts in a cheap spiral notebook to be

a fantastic stress reliever. I call it my Spew Journal. Once I get every annoyance, fear, worry, and rant out of my head and onto the page, I temporarily feel peace. I can't explain it. And, no, it's not a cure. The next morning I'll wake up and feel the anger all over again, but I jot it down and feel a little freer. Soon, the problem passes, or maybe I'm emotionally dealing with it better and no longer need to spew. Sometimes I'll just get sick of writing the same whiney story over and over. I'll tell myself to get over it already! Journaling. It's a good thing.

12. If the bitterness is keeping you up at night, make an extra effort to exercise during the day. It's a known stress reliever, and it makes you tired. Also, consider checking out the website, The Warm Milk Journal (www.thewarmmilkjournal.com),[9] which has hundreds of tips to reduce anxiety and reclaim your sleep.

Embrace Joy

Somewhere in the midst of avoiding bitterness, we have to make a conscious choice to embrace joy. I'm a work in progress with this one.

During a sports season, it's more difficult for me to embrace joy. But I have some tricks to refocus my mind and stay peaceful.

1. I practice gratitude that my child has been blessed with athletic ability.

2. When a situation seems unfair, I think of the kids who didn't make the team. Honestly, wouldn't any of them wish they had the chance to be in my child's shoes?

3. I keep the competitive claws sheathed. We give our joy away when we demand our kid be the best. Any thought that starts with *My kid is better than...*or *That kid isn't as good as...*will only fuel the competitive thinking that steals our joy. We're not *entitled* to the season we dream of for our kid.

4. If I'm at a game and I'm quickly losing it, I take a deep breath and picture a typical off-season day. This game doesn't matter as much as I think it does. I probably

won't even remember it a year from now.

5. I remind myself that my kid has a life outside of sports. This is only one part of him. Whatever happens during this game will not end his world. Or mine.

6. When I see my child working hard under tough circumstances, I make a special effort to celebrate it. I let her know I see how hard she's working.

7. If an unfair situation affects my kid's performance—let's face it, they usually play better when life is going their way—I try to shrug it off. I can find something to praise about the game, even if it's, "I was proud of how you cheered for Taylor."

8. I know this phase of my life is short-lived. I want to look back on these days and remember them fondly.

9. I think back on favorite memories of past seasons. Driving my son and his friends to games. Listening to my daughter and her friends singing and laughing on the way to tournaments. Spending time with my family, getting ice cream

afterward, and just being together. Those are the moments that bring me joy.

As long as my kids are in sports, I will strive to avoid bitterness and embrace joy. I'll fail sometimes. But that's okay, because I know I'm trying. I know what's important to me, and it's not that my kids are considered the best. To me they're the best simply because they're mine. And that's enough.

Truths to Take Away:

1. We're not entitled to have superstar athletes.

2. Life isn't fair. We can't control or influence every situation. Sometimes we have to just get through tough seasons, and it's hard.

3. Our kids need us to be adults. They soak in our attitudes, words, and actions, and we have an obligation to control ourselves even when it feels impossible.

4. Our children are stronger than we give them credit for. Tough situations can strengthen them. Encourage your kids to persevere and work hard.

CHAPTER TEN

Injuries, Slumps, And The Mental Game

"The Lord sustains them on their sickbed and restores them from their bed of illness." Psalm 41:3 (NIV)

You check the calendar. The season starts in two days! Will the team win their division this year? They've been practicing for weeks, and your son can't wait to play. Just then the door opens, and your son runs inside. He fell off his skateboard. His ankle is swelling. You hope and pray it's something minor, but X-rays and a doctor visit confirm the ankle is sprained. Instead of playing two days later, he's in a boot, on crutches, cheering for his team from the sidelines.

Why does this stuff happen?

If you've been involved in sports for a while, you're bound to hear of concussions, muscle strains, growth plate separations, sprains, fractures, and broken bones. Kids get injured all the time, and often they aren't even hurt during a game or practice. They were riding a scooter, jumping on a trampoline, or they slipped on a patch of ice.

Then there are slumps. No, your kid isn't on crutches or injured, but he's frustrated. For whatever reason your son has missed every field goal he's kicked in the past three football games. Or your daughter has missed every tennis serve this season. They're in a slump and no matter what they do, they can't seem to get out of it.

When your daughter is forced to sit on the sidelines due to a physical problem, her muscles are no longer growing stronger the way they were with regular practice. She's missing playing time, and this means she's losing an opportunity to get better. She's also no longer a key member of the team. It's not that she isn't accepted and supported by her teammates; she's not making an impact for them, so she's in the shadows.

When your son is going through a slump, the coach might work with him, give him a pep talk, or basically expect him to snap out of it. If the slump goes on for more than a few games, your son might be moved into another position with someone else taking his place. The team will be frustrated because he is costing them points and not helping them win. He, too, will feel resigned to the shadows.

Whether your child is on the sidelines with an injury or is going through a slump, her mental game is affected. Each day she's not practicing might fill her with determination to be better than ever when she's cleared, but there's also the worry that the team doesn't need her, that the other girl in her spot will keep it. She also might not be realistic about how her body has physically reacted to this forced rest. If she broke her leg and expects to run her personal best times at a track meet, she'll be in for an unwelcome surprise when her cast comes off and her muscles have atrophied.

And what about the one in the slump? The longer it goes on, the harder it is to get out of. Your enthusiastic son now dreads practices and games. He's unsure of himself, no longer bouncing out of his seat in his haste to get there. His teammates might begin to bully him, seizing their opportunity to act superior because they now see themselves as better players.

This is another area where parents feel helpless. We want to fix our kids. Get them out of the cast or slump ASAP. Some parents are tempted to ignore the doctor's orders and rely on how their daughter feels. The sprained elbow no longer hurts after two weeks? You tell her to go ahead and take the sling off. She can at least do some light workouts with her team. You conveniently ignore the doctor's orders to rest it for six weeks.

Not following doctor's orders can hurt your child. Her body is growing, and she needs a full healing period if she's going to recover. That being said, talk to your doctor about the injury. A broken bone is one thing, but muscle strain is another. For instance, our teenage daughter had shin splints and pain from muscle overuse during cross country. She had one race left in the season. The doctor advised her to avoid running for six weeks, but he also told her she could safely run the final race without permanently damaging her legs. She chose to compete, and immediately after, took a six-week break.

In the case of growth plates, broken bones, and other more serious injuries, ask yourself what is more important, your child playing the rest of the season or having a fully functional body the rest of her life?

During a slump, we stress out and pepper our kid with tips, extra practices at home, and any expert advice we can get our hands on. We fret, wondering if we were wrong all this time, and maybe he isn't cut out for the sport after all. If he could just kick *one* field goal, we know he'll snap out of it.

Slumps are trying on the child and the parents. Let me assure you of one thing. Your kid does *not* want to be in a slump. He is doing everything in his power to get out of it. This isn't about him not trying hard or ignoring instructions. For whatever reason, he's failing at something he's been able to do in the past, and it's scary.

My kids have been in slumps, and I've done everything a parent can do (and probably shouldn't do). I've tried to keep their spirits up. Talked to them about their form. Practiced at home. Discussed it with the coaches. You name it, I've tried it. I'd like to say I did this entirely out of love for them, but I'd be lying.

Sometimes we want our kids to get out of a slump for *us*. It goes back to the lie. We equate our kid's success with our own. When it seems as if they are failing, we feel like we're failing too.

So what can we do?

Be patient. Be supportive. It's normal for kids to get down when they're injured or in a slump, but discourage negativity. Let them know this is just a phase. They will heal. They will get out of the slump. Do a quick online search of top professional athletes; read a few interviews. Professional athletes are vocal about previous slumps and injuries. Share this information with your kids—let them know all athletes go through this at times. They aren't alone, and if they persevere, they'll get through it.

Don't let it affect how you treat them. They don't need your insecurity adding more tension to an already loaded situation. Too much pressure can lead to your kid engaging in risky behavior, like trying performance enhancement drugs or developing an eating disorder.

According to the http://www.mayoclinic.org/ article,

"Performance Enhancement Drugs and Teen Athletes,"[10] common reasons teens and tweens try performance enhancement drugs (PEDs) include pressure from parents or peers regarding their muscles or weight, the drive to gain a competitive edge, insecurity, and the desire to fit in with kids their age. Don't be afraid to have a conversation with your kids about how using PEDs is unhealthy, unethical, and the same as cheating. Lay out clear consequences (quitting the team, getting counseling, and so on) and follow through if your children fail to heed your rules.

Increasing body mass isn't the only way to gain an edge. Certain sports are more prone to rewarding athletes who are thin. In the article "Athletes and Eating Disorders,"[11] released by the National Eating Disorders Association, www.nationaleatingdisorders.org, sports such as wrestling, diving, running, and gymnastics emphasize body appearance and weight. This emphasis can put undo anxiety on athletes, propelling them to decrease their calorie intake and/or spend an excessive amount of time training. If you suspect your son or daughter may be overly occupied with losing weight in order to advance in a sport, please talk to him or her about it. Explain that growing and gaining weight are normal, healthy changes our bodies go through. An excellent resource regarding eating disorders and athletes is the _NEDA TOOLKIT for Coaches and Trainers_ published by the National Eating Disorders Association.[12] It's a downloadable/printable pdf booklet with an overview of eating disorders, prevention tips, personal stories, and many resources.

Whether your kids are struggling through an injury, in a slump, or on the slippery-slope of risky behavior, their mental game is affected.

So what if your daughter misses half the season with a bad knee? She'll heal and be back at it when she's ready. Since there's not much you or your son can do about a slump, just encourage him to keep trying, to keep doing his best. And if you suspect your kids are feeling the pressure to perform to the point they're taking PEDs or developing an eating disorder, get them professional help.

Most of all, during the tough times, make sure you're emotionally supporting your children, not pressuring them. That's what they really need.

Truths to Take Away:

1. A healthy body is more important than the current sport season.

2. Slumps do not last forever.

3. This sport is not a life or death situation, so don't act as if a slump or injury is the end of the world.

CHAPTER ELEVEN

The Off-Season

"By the seventh day God had finished the work he had been doing; so on the seventh day he rested from all his work." Genesis 2:2 (NIV)

Ahh...the off-season. A chance to slow down, regroup and prepare for next year. It's a little bittersweet. I enjoy watching my kids play sports, and I also have fun hanging out with other parents on a regular basis. That being said, a nice long break from the busy schedule, stress, and drama is always welcome.

What Do Your Kids Want?

Whether the season ended on a high note or a sour one, my husband and I touch base with our kids a week or two after the final game. We can probably guess how they feel, but it's important to get their input so there aren't any needless misunderstandings.

These are the questions we tend to ask.

Do you still want to play?

Is this team a good fit or do you want to try out for a different one?

What were you good at?

What skills do need to work on?

If your child no longer wants to play, ask him why. Sometimes it's a clear, easy decision for everyone involved. He tried a sport, didn't like it, wasn't good at it, wasn't improving, and wants out. In this case, honor his decision, and encourage him to try something else.

Sometimes a kid loves a sport but gets down on herself for whatever reason. The season ends, and she says she doesn't want to play anymore. If she's angry and defensive, encourage her to explain what made her attitude change. Some kids are more introverted than others, and your child might struggle to put the reason into words. Or she could be a perfectionist, scared of letting her coach or you down and unable to verbalize these fears.

Don't be afraid to remind her she couldn't wait to play before the season started. If she responds with comments such as she isn't good, doesn't like so-and-so, or the coach hates her, do your best to listen without adding anything. I know—this is difficult! But her opinion matters, and if you treat her with respect, she'll be more likely to make wise decisions.

You might disagree with everything she's saying. You may be shaking your head, thinking she's delusional. Try your best to not be dismissive or disdainful. Her feelings are real and based on something she believes, whether true or not.

This is a good time to ask if things were different, would she still want to play. Use the argument she gave you.

If you *were* good, would you still want to play?

If such-and-such *wasn't* a jerk, would you still want to play?

If the coach *didn't* hate you, would you still want to play?

Kids can be quick to take the easy way out—don't we all want to avoid pain? But it isn't always in their best interests.

If your child would still want to play if "things were different," discuss ways for the situation to change. Does anyone offer private lessons in the off-season? Maybe a training program would boost her confidence. Explore the possibilities, but don't feel obligated to spend money on anything. Weigh the pros and cons of trying out for a different team/switching facilities. If a teammate has been on her nerves, help her focus on the kids she *does* like. It's easy to home in on the one negative person while conveniently forgetting the dozen others who make us feel accepted.

Staying Healthy

If the season ended and your child can't wait to play next season, use the off-season wisely. It's called the off-season for a reason—let their poor bodies rest!

Recent studies have shown that kids are more prone to injury and burnout if they compete in a sport year-round. The American Medical Society for Sports Medicine has an excellent position statement on the subject. You can find "Overuse Injuries and Burnout in Youth Sports (2014)" on their website under the publications tab (www.amssm.org/publications.html).[13]

We know many people who have children playing in multiple sports year-round. One of their kids might play on travel teams for volleyball and basketball as well as competing in a swim league. Their other child might play travel basketball, compete in track, and play football. These are a lot of sports for one family to deal with. Your family will have to decide how much is too much. Some families thrive on this, and others need more downtime. Whether you choose to allow your kids to play multiple sports throughout the year or to focus on one is up to you.

Making The Most Of The Off-Season

Kids need a break from the mental and physical stress of demanding sports. Encourage them to stay in shape during the off-season with activities that don't strain their overworked muscles. The key to this time is allowing their bodies to rest, to grow, and to heal from the wear and tear of the previous season. For example: A volleyball player might try swimming. A basketball player could sign up for kick-boxing. A cross country runner can lift weights. A football player can build core strength with yoga.

The goal is for them to work their muscles in a different way than they do during the season.

Let them explore other interests. This is a good time to try non-athletic pursuits like drawing, reading, playing a new video game, singing, making home movies, or learning to play an instrument. Sports can feel all-consuming. Having other interests can be a welcome change from the intensity of competitive sports.

Parents can use the off-season to their advantage, too. I always have less anxiety in general between seasons. Talk to your significant other about the practical aspects. If one of you always drives to and from practices, is this still feasible? Is there anything you can do to make game days less hectic? Are your kids forgetting pieces of their uniform on a weekly basis? Can you help them organize their sports' equipment and uniforms to avoid last minute problems in the future?

What about the costs? Can you still afford this sport? Having a frank discussion helps douse a potentially tense situation.

All these extra demands on our time are difficult, and when there's a chronic wail of "I can't find my shorts/cleats/helmet," or if Mom is racing home from work to get dear daughter to dance on time every Tuesday and Thursday while Dad has more flex time, resentments flare. Maybe Dad needs to drive her to dance these days, or maybe you'll come up with another solution that neither of you previously considered. Communication is key, and between seasons is the ideal time to have these discussions. I've included a bonus chapter at the end of the book with practical solutions to these and other everyday sports problems.

If there's one thing to do in the off-season, it's this. Enjoy it!

Truths to Take Away:

1. Year round training in one sport could lead to overuse injuries and burnout. Encourage your children to pursue other interests during the off-season.

2. The off-season is the ideal time to have a family discussion about any practical matters concerning the sport.

CHAPTER TWELVE

Is It Time To Quit?

"Show me your ways, Lord, teach me your paths."
Psalm 25:4 (NIV)

*Q*uit? What kind of crazy talk is that?

When it comes to our kids, this four-letter word might be the one Americans hate the most. We shudder as memories of our parents spinning tales about our tough ancestors roar in our heads. *If Great-Grandpa Rupert could chop down ten trees for firewood, walk barefoot through three miles of snow, and hunt a moose in time for dinner at the age of fifteen, surely my daughter can suck it up and play golf for one more season.*

Sometimes quitting is the right thing to do. Even if Great-Grandpa Rupert wrestled a bear after hunting the moose.

Surviving A Bad Experience

In the name of full disclosure, our house rule is that *no one* is allowed to quit a sport mid-season. If you commit to something, you must see it through until the current season ends. Obviously, if our child is in danger or in a situation where our family's morals are being compromised, quitting would be mandatory immediately. But other than that, quitting before the season ends is not permitted.

My husband and I believe it's important for our kids to learn they will survive a bad experience in life. Eight weeks left of being on a team you loathe? Deal with it. Six weeks of intense workouts with coaches who never let you play? You're strong enough to see it through. Whine if you have to, but you'll be at every practice and every game, and you will survive.

Life isn't always easy.

Wait—is life ever easy?

I don't know. Even when everything seems to be going my way, there's some difficulty to deal with.

Finishing a rough season nourishes survival skills, and even if our kids don't appreciate them now, someday, they will need these skills.

As children we get stuck with mean team-mates; as adults we get stuck with awful coworkers. We can't quit our job every time we hate it, nor should we. Life has an ebb and flow, and the miserable job might become a great one in six months when the work bully quits. Or we might hang on to our paying job while looking for a better one. If our kids quit everything that doesn't meet their expectations, they won't develop the patience and fortitude needed in life.

However, if our kids tried a sport and hated it, at the end of the season they are allowed to quit. They survived the experience and, hopefully, developed resilience to navigate future unpleasant situations.

Factors To Consider Before Quitting

A lot of factors should be considered before allowing your child to quit a sport. Do any of these sound familiar?

- The team lost the past twenty games they played.
- Your daughter was benched for half the season.
- Your son keeps getting reinjured.

- The practices and games have eaten up every free moment of your family time.
- You lost your job and have to find ways to stretch your finances.
- Your daughter's anxiety levels are through the roof—stomachaches, headaches, worrying about games.
- Your son shows zero aptitude for the sport and makes no improvement as the season progresses. As a result, he doesn't like playing and wants out.
- Your daughter has no enthusiasm for practices or games. She just isn't having fun.

Yes, it might be time to quit.

Or it might be time to regroup and persevere.

How do you know if it's time to quit or if your kid should hang in there?

Slogging through a losing season is *not* an indicator that your child should quit a sport. If your daughter likes her teammates, feels good about herself, and genuinely enjoys playing, then who cares if they consistently lose? You might shiver as you look back on these years with all the stomachache-inducing losses, but she'll likely remember them as super fun doing what she loved with her friends.

On the other hand if your daughter is frustrated at always losing, developing lazy habits due to the influence of her teammates, or not growing as a player, it might be time for her to quit and try out for another team.

What about when your daughter is benched? Is that grounds for quitting? Not necessarily. Be honest. Did she have a bad attitude? Was her effort lacking? Are the other kids on the team simply better players? If she still likes the sport, encourage her to stick with it, to try hard, and to be a good teammate. This might be the time to look at different teams where she can get more playing time.

Moving on to injuries. If your kid loves a sport but continues to injure the same body part over and over, I would highly recommend taking time off to recover. His body is too important. You don't want him living with lifelong pain, weakness, or a permanent injury. Let his body heal, and I'm not talking about two weeks. Let it heal all the way. Let it get strong. Then decide if it's worth going back to the sport. And please get medical help if your child gets a concussion. This is his brain. Listen to the doctor's advice.

What about time and money? When you're stretched so thin you're about to snap, seriously consider dropping sports. There is no law stating parents have to allow their kids to play. Maybe a season off is exactly what your family needs in this time of life. Have an honest conversation with everyone in the family and discuss why you're making the decision. Also, make every effort for your kids to stay active. If there are free, local activities, try to get them involved. And weather permitting, get outside together. Take walks, shoot some hoops, ride bikes, play a little tennis. Have some fun.

What if your kid desperately wants to play basketball, but his first season was a personal disaster? He had no coordination, missed every shot the few times he did play, and never seemed to progress? Well, does he still want to play? If he does, then you might have to swallow your parent pride and get your cheering gloves on. One of the biggest mistakes parents make is discouraging our kids from challenging themselves through embarrassing or difficult situations. If your kid is willing to be on the team, I say let him. Who knows? His passion may make him a great player down the line.

Anxiety comes naturally with sports, but when the anxiety is excessive—it's causing your child to be physically ill or unusually fearful—please allow her to quit. Playing a sport should not cause an ulcer.

Most experts will disagree with me on the next point, so please take it with a grain of salt. If your kid shows no enthusiasm and isn't having fun, is it time to quit? The experts say, yes, if your child isn't having fun, it's time to quit. I stand by my opinion that sports are supposed to be fun. However, I think there are times when a kid isn't having fun that it's *not okay* for him to quit. Bear with me as I try to explain.

Our society believes happiness is something to always strive for, a personal right. But kids aren't always going to be happy. Some of the things they don't enjoy are necessary parts of their journey to becoming responsible adults.

Do your kids have fun washing the dishes? Doing homework? Walking the dog in the rain? Spending hard-earned money to replace something they broke? Hanging out at a nursing home with their elderly grandparent? Getting up early for church? I'm sure your kids enjoy some of those things and grumble at others. Sometimes quitting is an escape that isn't in your child's best interests, and other times it's the right thing to do.

Here are a few scenarios of when you should let your child quit or when you should encourage him to press on.

Your daughter decided to try basketball. You signed her up for a local recreational league. The first week she bounced home full of excitement. She liked the coach, had a great time learning new skills, and became friends with another girl on the team. By week three, your daughter shrugged when you asked her how it was going. She began complaining her back hurt. Asked if she could skip practice. You attended the first game, and your heart sank as she sat on the bench, not playing once. During a practice or two, you perched on the bleachers, and it was clear your daughter had no natural talent at the sport. Also, the best players were getting a lot of encouragement from the coaches, but the less skilled ones were either ignored or getting yelled at. When the season is over, your daughter says she doesn't want to play anymore.

Do you let her quit?

Absolutely. It's okay to try something and later decide it isn't your thing. But ask her if she is still interested in learning how to play basketball. If she is, maybe you could find a different team or enroll her in a summer basketball camp. If she wants nothing to do with basketball, praise her for trying something new and give her your blessing to quit.

On the other hand, your son has wrestled for two years. He's pretty good at it and in the past has enjoyed it. This was his first year wrestling for the junior varsity team in high school. He went through a growth spurt and no longer wrestled in the weight group he previously excelled in. He also had a new coach, different training techniques, and unfamiliar kids to compete against. The season didn't go well, and he often came home complaining. He admitted he wasn't very good, and his record reflected it. When the season is over, he announces he's done wrestling.

Do you let him quit?

Maybe. Maybe not.

Obviously, he didn't have fun this year. But how much of that was due to the onslaught of changes in his life? When kids are growing, they struggle with emotions, coordination, and even physical pain. Moving from junior high to high school brings additional challenges. Add a new coach, different training methods, and competing against a different set of kids? It's stressful for the best athletes.

Encourage your son to give wrestling another year before quitting. I'd hate to see him give up on something he truly enjoys just because he had a bad year. Sports don't always go smoothly. By supporting him to push forward and to not let these things stop him, you're telling him, "Hey, I believe in you, and I want you to believe in yourself, too."

Quitting a sport causes a long-term effect. Be honest with him. Explain that if he quits now, he could be denying himself opportunities to continue the sport in the future.

Is This In My Child's Best Interests?

Parents get extremely invested in youth sports. We tell our friends when Johnny made the hockey team or Susie spiked the winning point in her volleyball game. Our social life is affected by sports. It can be fun to hang out with parents on the bleachers. We reap social benefits by having our kids play sports.

Unfortunately, we might place our own needs above our children's when it comes to quitting.

If your child hates playing soccer but you refuse to listen because you enjoy telling people your son is on an all-star team or your social life revolves around the other parents on the team, take a hard look at yourself. Let him quit.

If your daughter mentions skipping cheerleading tryouts this year because she's constantly pressured to drink alcohol at the parties all the football players and cheerleaders attend, put your bragging rights aside. Gracefully give up your spot on the bleachers because your daughter's safety is more important than your identity as a cheerleader mom. You may be thinking, *Just tell your daughter not to go to the parties.* That is an option, but maybe being surrounded by a culture that celebrates doing things against your daughter's code of ethics isn't good for her, and she knows it. Discuss with her how to handle the situation. Hopefully, you'll both come up with a solution that keeps her safe, even if she stays on the team.

The bottom line about sports is they aren't about us. They're about our kids.

If your child wants to quit a sport, don't rush into saying yes or no. There are so many factors in making this decision. Only you know the circumstances. What is your gut telling you? Have you listened to your child's reasoning? How does your spouse feel?

Ask yourself what is the worst thing that could happen if your child quits?

What's the best thing that could happen?

Quitting a sport now doesn't mean your child will never play it again. She might surprise you by taking a season off and missing it. Maybe she'll try out again in two years. Maybe not. But life will go on, and your family will be okay. Before making any decisions, ask your child to pray about it. And of course, parents need to pray about it, also.

Truths to Take Away:

1. Excessive anxiety is a sign your child should step away from a sport.

2. Persevering through a lousy, depressing, mediocre, or just plain awful season will not destroy your child. Pushing through hard times builds resilience. However, don't pressure your kid to continue playing a sport he hates.

3. The sport isn't about you. It's about your child.

CHAPTER THIRTEEN

Affirmations For The Tough Games

"Yes, my soul, find rest in God; my hope comes from him." Psalm 62:5 (NIV)

No matter how hard you try to keep your cool, there will be times when you lose it. The bad call. The missed opportunity. Another parent causing a ruckus. You might have a serene smile on your face as you're mentally flipping out. Maybe you're pacing behind the bleachers, furious at what's happening, or clenching your teeth, trying not to shout at the parent who just won't stop complaining.

You're going to have tough games.

I've had them, and I continue to have them. They come with the territory.

As I've mentioned repeatedly, I struggle to maintain a good attitude, to keep the focus on my kids, to remember the big picture instead of the present moment. I'm a work-in-progress, and I always will be. That being said, I no longer arrive at one of my kids' sporting events without being prepared. I know what I signed up for, and it isn't all happiness and bliss.

I've created a list of affirmations for the tough games. You can print them out (go to my website, jillkemerer.com/books/game-on/, for the downloadable/printable version) to keep in your purse or pocket or you can copy/paste the list into a note on your phone.

The Affirmations

1. This game will not last forever.
2. My child is so much more than a player on this team.
3. Life isn't about who is best. It's about doing your best.
4. Will this matter in a week? A year? Ten years?
5. I can rise above my feelings in this moment.
6. Breathe. My physical state affects my mental state.

7. I can pray about this situation.
8. I can use this opportunity to be a positive influence.
9. I don't need to be afraid.
10. God loves me.
11. God loves my child.
12. God is using this experience for my good and the good of my child.
13. I am self-disciplined and will control myself.
14. I am thankful in all circumstances.
15. I trust God right now.

Breaking Them Down

Sure, a few affirmations are nice and all, but do they work? If you only read them or recite them, they might not do you much good. To be effective, you have to actually believe them. And that's why we're looking at each one in depth.

1. This game will not last forever.

I hope this one isn't hard to believe. Some games feel endless, but they all do, indeed, end. This one will, too. And if this game won't last forever, whatever you're feeling won't either.

2. My child is so much more than a player on this team.

Remind yourself of the list you made with five things you're proud of concerning your child. Your kid isn't defined by a sport. Neither are you.

3. Life isn't about who is best. It's about doing your best.

Being the best is a fleeting thing. Records are made, then broken. Today's superstar might not even play in another year or two. The world is filled with underdog stories. Athletes who started out with average talent work hard to reach the top.

4. Will this matter in a week? A year? Ten years?

If your daughter choked during the state golf tournament, yes, it will matter in a week. The tougher the loss, the longer it takes to get over. But in a year? Probably not. In ten years? She's moved on with her life. This game or practice isn't all that important in the grand scheme of things.

5. I can rise above my feelings in this moment.

Feel that burning resentment in your chest as the parent of Miss Star Player brags about her dear daughter? The girl who has never, ever sat out on the bench even though she's tripping over herself up and down the court? Picture yourself somewhere else. Anywhere else. Maybe you're on a beach reading a novel. Maybe you're on the porch of a log cabin, drinking coffee and admiring the view of the mountains. If mentally exiting the game isn't possible, excuse yourself and sit or stand somewhere else. Remind yourself you're not trapped. You're blessed to have a child with athletic ability, and you're blessed to be watching her play.

6. Breathe. My physical state affects my mental state.

Another nasty side effect of stress is our fight-or-flight response. When you're upset, you're probably breathing shallowly and don't even realize it. Force yourself to take long, deep breaths. Count to four on the inhalation, hold for a few counts, and slowly release the breath. Repeat this until your breathing is normal. Are your hands clenched? Your shoulders rigid? Flex your hands, stretch your neck to the side. Releasing your physical tension subdues the internal tension.

7. I can pray about this situation.

I constantly rely on God's power and love to see me through life. Pray for God to give you the peace He promises in Philippians 4:7 "And the peace of God, which transcends all understanding, will guard your hearts and your minds in Christ Jesus." Go ahead and pray for a good outcome for your child, too, but remember, God knows what's best for our kids and some days aren't going to turn out the way we'd like.

8. I can use this opportunity to be a positive influence.

When everyone around you is dissolving into a petty, argumentative, screaming mob, you do not have to join in. You don't even have to respond to it. Keep your words kind, your body language relaxed. Group behavior is contagious. Don't follow the crowd.

9. I don't need to be afraid.

Remember, this isn't a gladiator game. This sport doesn't involve a fight to the death. There will be a winner and a loser. Both teams will move on with their lives, and you don't need to fear the outcome.

10. God loves me.

When our kids' sports don't go the way we hoped, we wonder why. Is God punishing them? Punishing us? He isn't. He loves you. He loves your children. We don't know why painful things happen, but they aren't due to some vindictive deity. God is love. He sent His Son to die on the cross so you will spend eternity with Him in heaven. That's love.

11. God loves my child.

You know how much you love your child? How you sacrifice and dream and hope your baby has a good life? God loves your kid even more than you do. If that doesn't reassure you, what will?

12. God is using this experience for my good and the good of my child.

You might never know why this experience is happening, but you can be sure God will work it out for your child's good. The experience itself might be kick-in-the-gut-painful, and you might never recognize how it positively shapes your child, but it will. God promises in Romans 8:28 "And we know that in all things God works for the good of those who love him, who have been called according to his purpose."

13. I am self-disciplined and will control myself.

I am the adult. The parent. The role model. I will act like it.

14. I am thankful in all circumstances.

All circumstances? Surely, not in *this* one. Yes, even in this circumstance you can find something to be thankful for. Your child is alive.

You're alive. The seasons keep changing, the earth keeps spinning. You're not in prison; you're free to come to practices and games. What a blessing! You will eat today. You'll have something to wear, somewhere to sleep, and hopefully you'll have a friend or two. We have so much to be thankful for, but we ignore the obvious to focus on what we don't have. We refuse to be happy with the million and one other things we're blessed with because we can only concentrate on the issue in front of us.

15. I trust God right now.

This is the heart of most of my problems. I see things not going my way, and instead of trusting God will work it all out for my good, I assume He's not trustworthy. What needless worrying and anxiety I experience because of this. God is trustworthy. Every moment. Every day. All the time.

Bible Passages

The following Bible passages bring me reassurance. I hope they reassure you, too. You can download the complete list from my website at jillkemerer.com/books/game-on/.

- Psalm 37:7 (NIV) "Be still before the Lord and wait patiently for him; do not fret when people succeed in their ways, when they carry out their wicked schemes."

- Luke 12:24 (NIV) "Consider the ravens: They do not sow or reap, they have no storeroom or barn; yet God feeds them. And how much more valuable you are than birds!"

- 1 Corinthians 15:58 (NIV) "Therefore my dear brothers and sisters, stand firm. Let nothing move you. Always give yourself fully to the work of the Lord, because you know that your labor in the Lord is not in vain."

- Ecclesiastes 3:1 (NIV) "There is a time for everything, and a season for every activity under the heavens:"

- Psalm 40:2 (NIV) "He lifted me out of the slimy pit, out of the mud and mire; he set my foot on a rock and gave me a firm place to stand."

- Psalm 62:5 (NIV) "Yes, my soul, find rest in God; my hope comes from him."

- James 1:5 (NIV) "If any of you lacks wisdom, you should ask God, who gives generously to all without finding fault, and it will be given to you."

- Matthew 5:16 (NIV) "In the same way, let your light shine before others, that they may see your good deeds and glorify your Father in heaven."
- Leviticus 26:6 (NIV) "I will grant peace in the land, and you will lie down and no one will make you afraid. I will remove wild beasts from the land, and the sword will not pass through your country."
- Psalm 40:1 (NIV) "I waited patiently for the Lord; he turned to me and heard my cry."
- Romans 8:38-39 (NIV) "For I am convinced that neither death nor life, neither angels nor demons, neither the present nor the future, nor any powers, neither height nor depth, nor anything else in all creation, will be able to separate us from the love of God that is in Christ Jesus our Lord."
- Romans 8:28 (NIV) "And we know that in all things God works for the good of those who love him, who have been called according to his purpose."
- 2 Timothy 1:7 (NIV) "For the Spirit God gave us does not make us timid, but gives us power, love and self-discipline."

- 1 Thessalonians 5:16-18 (NIV) "Rejoice always, pray continually, give thanks in all circumstances; for this is God's will for you in Christ Jesus."
- 2 Corinthians 4:18 (NIV) "So we fix our eyes not on what is seen, but on what is unseen, since what is seen is temporary, but what is unseen is eternal."

Truths to Take Away:

1. We are not powerless on the sidelines. Instead of worrying, screaming, coaching, or fretting, read through the affirmations. Be aware of your physical responses. Get away from people who are stressing you out.

2. Arriving at the game full of optimism is great, but have a mental plan in place in case your kid plays poorly, the team loses, or other parents push your buttons.

Final Thoughts

Youth sports are complicated and competitive. What we hope will be a fun experience often puts enormous pressure on us and our children. One minute we're relieved and happy our daughter made the team, the next we're full of anxiety about her performance. Politics seem unfair, unethical, and unappealing, but we wonder if we're hurting our children by not playing the political game.

We're surrounded by a sports-crazy culture, and it's difficult not to buy into the lie that our kids' success is ours, too. If we've never considered why we have our children play sports, we settle for society's reasons, and they don't always mesh with our personal values. We drift toward poor behavior in an attempt to shield our kids from the inequalities present in youth sports.

But rather than reciting socially acceptable reasons about why we have our children playing sports, we can define our own reasons. In doing so, we break the grip of needing our kids to be the best. We no longer pressure them to win no matter the cost or point to a spot on the varsity team or an athletic scholarship as ultimate goals. Our kids might go on to play at higher levels, but they'll understand their self-worth is not wrapped up in their performance on the field. And we'll understand ours isn't either.

Yes, we'll feel anxiety along the way. We'll revert to falsely believing their success is our success. We'll fret when they're injured or in a slump. We'll fume when politics hurt them.

I hope we'll remind ourselves often of our own accomplishments and have a larger view of our kids' talents. Sports are just a part of their lives, and by modeling ethical behavior, we're showing our kids how to grow up to be people with integrity. When we allow them to struggle and don't let them quit for minor reasons, we're telling them they can handle tough seasons. They start to understand they're stronger than they thought. This strength will be tested as they get older, and if they continue to press forward even when it's hard, they'll gain a true and lasting confidence in themselves.

So when our kids don't get equal playing time or the positions they deserve, instead of stewing in bitterness, we can turn to God and trust Him. He loves us. He loves our kids. We'll still feel anxiety, but we can work hard to not let it overtake our lives.

In ten years, twenty years, fifty years, I hope we'll look back on these seasons and be proud of our behavior and see that our kids really did turn out okay despite the challenges they faced in sports.

Let's be lights in this dark world. Let's embrace joy. Let's be the parents our kids need.

And let's enjoy every minute of the ride.

Practical Matters And Fundraising

"Commit to the Lord whatever you do, and he will establish your plans." Proverbs 16:3 (NIV)

This chapter is full of tricks and tips I've learned over the years. I'm always picking up new ideas from blogs, Pinterest, Facebook, and other parents. Whether it's dealing with a crazy schedule, packing the car, carpooling, fundraising, uniform care, or streamlining life, I look for ways to make it all easier.

First, let me warn you, I'm a list person. I love my day planner. I also use the Evernote app, the Notes feature, and my iPhone's calendar to keep track of practices, instructions from coaches, the game schedule, and anything else related to sports. What works for me might not work for you. My advice? Try new systems until you find one you like. Then stick with it!

In the meantime, let's talk about practical matters.

Money

Most sports involve money. Even if your child is playing a free sport through school, money will be involved. Football players need cleats and gear. Volleyball players need knee-pads, socks, and headbands. Cross country runners require long-distance running shoes. Then there are hockey players—ouch!—I feel for you. Hockey might be the most expensive sport out there!

A lot of parents are not only paying for gear or clothing items, they're also paying expensive fees for their kids to play.

Some parents have enough wiggle room in the budget to pay for these expenses when they come up. For those who don't, I suggest sitting down once a year and adding up all the projected costs for every sport your children play during the year. What goes on this list? Any team fees (annual fees, monthly dance lessons), any additional fees you know of (an organization fee, off-season practice facility), equipment (shoulder pads, hockey stick, baseball bat), athletic clothing (cleats, running shoes, leotards, warm-ups), tournament costs (hotel room, transportation, meals, kennel for pets while you're gone), special costs (private lessons, batting cages, the driving range), and possible fundraising costs (sponsoring the team, purchasing items the team sells in a fundraiser).

The list you come up with will either seem overwhelming and you'll hyperventilate, or it will be so suspiciously low, you'll realize you forgot half the expenses. Once you're sure you've listed most, if not all, of the costs involved, add everything up for *each* sport. If you have more than one child, do the same for all your kids. Keep the totals for each sport separate. Tally the costs for each child (example: Susie does competitive dance and volleyball, Johnny plays hockey, runs track, and plays on a travel basketball team). After you have individual totals for your kids, you can add the costs of all the sports for a grand total.

These lists should be insightful. If you're spending twice as much on Susie's extracurricular activities than you are on Johnny's, and you're struggling financially, it might make sense to ask Susie to drop one of her activities. You can show her the reality of the expenses to take some of the emotional heat out of it. If you hear, "But Johnny plays three sports," you can calmly explain that Johnny's sports add up to half the costs of her two activities. Math doesn't lie. Let it be your ally.

Once you've decided what activities your family can afford, add up all the costs from these sports again. You can save for the expenses in a number of ways. One method is to divide the grand total by twelve and, each month, set the money aside either in a savings account or an envelope. If that isn't possible and you typically get a bonus, tax return, or other infrequent source of income, set the full amount (or as much as you can) aside then. If you're squinting at the total and still at a loss for how you could possibly pay for it all, you might need to make a few more tough decisions.

Sports are stressful enough. Worrying about how we're going to pay for them shouldn't keep us up at night. Take a long, hard look at your budget. Is there somewhere you can cut back to find the funds? Is it worth looking into a less expensive league? Is it time for your kid to quit one or more sports?

You'll probably feel guilty. I feel guilty about all kinds of things on a regular basis. But that's part of parenting. Making tough choices for the good of your family. Everyone's financial picture is different. Only you can decide what's best for you.

Time

The next big issue parents come up against is time. Practices and games aren't always convenient. Maybe your daughter's dance lessons are scheduled on Tuesdays and Thursdays from four to six, but you and your spouse work until five-thirty. Or your son's ice time for hockey is at five in the morning twenty minutes away. The lacrosse tournament two hundred miles from home starts Friday morning and ends on Sunday. For dual income parents, these logistics can be a nightmare. They aren't any fun for families with stay-at-home parents, either. Add the other practices and games, and it's enough to make you crawl into bed and hide.

Since I've been shuttling kids to practices, games, and tournaments for years, I've come to believe the single best thing parents can do is carpool. At the beginning of each season, ask the coach for a parent roster with contact information. Call or email the list to see if anyone lives nearby who wants to carpool. Maybe one parent takes the kids to practices while another drives them home. Maybe you're "on" one week and "off" the next. Maybe four or five of you live near each other and don't even realize it. Whether you rely on one person occasionally or split duties with five other parents, you'll take a huge stress off your life. Frankly, I'm a fan of adding as many parents as possible to my phone's contact list. You never know when you might need one of them.

What if you don't know any of the parents and you feel uncomfortable approaching them? Make an effort to get to know them at games and practices. Casually mention exchanging contact information *just in case*. If an emergency comes up and you can't pick up your child, it's a lifesaver to be able to text other parents who might be able to help. Of course, you should be willing to help them in return. This is a give and take arrangement, not a one-sided affair.

A few notes about carpooling. Do everything you can to divide responsibilities equally. If one parent is able and willing to drive a significant amount more than the others, show your appreciation with a thank you. This person is making your life easier. What a blessing! Also, divorced parents, make sure your carpool drivers know which house your child is being picked up or dropped off to for each practice and game.

Whether you choose to carpool or not, plan ahead for the season. As soon as you get practice and game schedules, add them to your calendar. Then sit down and figure out how you'll get your kids to them. If you're dealing with multiple children in sports at the same time, get all the schedules in front of you.

Are you a single parent? Do you have anyone (grandparent, close friend, sibling) who could help you out with practices and games? If you know there might be times your child simply will not have a way to make it to practice, talk to the coach about this. Maybe a solution will come up you didn't expect.

Two-income parents, get the schedules in front of you and take time to hash out a plan. These meetings can get ugly, so do everything in your power to keep it friendly. Does one of you have more flexibility than the other? Looking over the schedule, are there any times either of you absolutely cannot make a

game/practice/tournament because of a mandatory work responsibility? Write this information down. Then divvy up who is responsible
for particular days/times. Write down who is
driving when. Either post this on a family calendar where everyone can see it or add it to an
online calendar you can share with your family.

As with all things home-life related, driving
the children to and from sports isn't going to
turn out 50/50. Accept it and move on. You're
doing this for your kids. Just one more sacrifice
in a long line of them. If you get hung up on
making everything equal, you'll just grow re-
sentful.

Households with stay-at-home parents, don't
assume the stay-at-home spouse is automatically
responsible for the transportation to all practices and games. Yes, the at-home parent has more
flexibility and will probably take on the majority of driving responsibilities, but sit down with
the schedules and figure out ways for both parents to contribute. I'm a work-from-home mom.
I've always been the main driver for our kids'
sports, but this takes valuable time away from
my job. My husband's job has always been demanding with long hours. He drives when he
can, but I've learned to rely on carpooling more

than anything else. When I do drive to practices and games, I often bring my laptop or manuscripts with me. During pre-game warm-ups, I might work in the car or on the bleachers. It's not ideal, but modern problems require modern solutions. I work where and when I can.

Practices

In my house, the most common problems regarding practices are failing to leave on time, missing clothing or gear, and being hungry with no time to eat. My kids need adequate time to get ready. Five minutes just doesn't cut it when we're talking about changing clothes, grabbing a water bottle, finding the lost hat/headband/socks, throwing the duffel bag in the trunk, and inhaling a snack. We aim to get to practices ten minutes early. If too many days go by with a kid frantically looking for a missing kneepad, I make changes. This isn't a time issue, it's an organization issue.

We try to implement systems for uniforms, practice gear, and equipment. I say try, because, let's face it, life is messy. It would be so lovely to live in a world where I explained the importance of putting things away and my kids automatically *put things away* from that point on, but it doesn't happen. We tell our kids to keep their clean uniforms and practice clothes in the same spot so they're easy to find. We also make them store their gear in the same place in the garage. There's nothing more frustrating than already being late and driving five minutes down the road to hear, "I forgot my—" you fill in the blank.

If you and your child are regularly rushing around in a tizzy trying to find a helmet or jersey, spend a few minutes brainstorming ways to fix the problem. Is there a dedicated space in your house/apartment/garage for your children's equipment? Does the gear sprawl everywhere? Could you purchase an inexpensive bin for it?

Is the problem bigger due to multiple kids in various sports? Look into a locker or cubby system. Even a sturdy rack of shelves could solve the issue. Help your kids by providing them a place to store their sports equipment.

Have your children pick a spot to keep their uniform pieces together. Maybe clean uniforms go directly into a duffel bag or get folded and set on top of their dresser. Some kids are natural organizers and others are free spirits who know where things are in a way you might not understand. If your messy child never puts uniforms away, but you don't have to reprimand him for not having his entire uniform, let go of the need to be neat. He obviously has a handle on the issue.

Maybe you're the more free-spirited person and your child is the neat freak. You don't understand why she gets so bent out of shape when you leave her uniform in the dryer or toss it in the corner with the other clean clothes. One solution would be for you to tell her when the uniform is clean so she can put it away. Another would be for you to let her fold and organize her uniform herself. Respect each other, and you'll be fine.

If you're struggling to leave on time, try using an alarm. I'm notorious for trying to get one more thing done, but I underestimate how long this one thing will take me. Set a timer fifteen minutes before you need to leave. Remind your child you're leaving in fifteen minutes. Then set another timer for five minutes before you need to leave. When this alarm goes off, put on your shoes, find your keys, and head to the door.

Food

Why do games and practices fall at such inconvenient times?

Does this sound familiar? Practice is from 5:30-7:30pm. *Well, that doesn't sound so bad.* Until you realize you'll have to leave by 5:10pm to get your daughter to the soccer fields, and it takes her fifteen minutes to get ready before you take her. Hmm...when is your kid supposed to eat? At 4:30pm? Seems awfully early. But if you wait until after practice, you're looking at 8:00pm.

How do parents prepare these meals? Cook at four in the afternoon? Reheat dinner at eight?

Meal planning around sports is tough. I rely on convenient meals for those days. I have a shortlist of quick and easy dinners to throw together. Sometimes I make double batches of freezer items like lasagna to thaw on game days. I also use my slow cooker. It's simple to throw pulled-pork sandwiches together or to serve a hearty stew with some bread. We try not to rely on fast food too much because it gets expensive and isn't very healthy. But, in the middle of a travel ball season when we're rocking three games a week and more games on the weekend, fast food happens. That's life.

We also buy bulk snack items. Get the multi-pack of yogurt, the 24-pack of water, the big box of granola bars. Buy string cheese, hummus and pita chips, fruit, and anything healthy-ish that's easy to grab and run. Sometimes your kid won't be able to eat much before a big game. Nerves are real. Make peace with the fact she'll eat afterward.

Another option is to have your kids eat a few mini-meals. They can eat a few snacks on the above list before the game or practice and have their main course after.

Depending on the sport, have your kids pack small coolers to stay hydrated. A reusable insulated lunch box works well. They can fit a freezer pack and a few water bottles in there. If games are in the summer, you might want to invest in a cooling neck wrap. Add water, snap them, and the wrap stays cool for a few hours. You can find them at a local superstore or building center.

Waiting

Parents with kids in sports practically live in their vehicles. Often, the players have to arrive an hour early for a game. Or practice is two hours, but you don't want to waste time driving home only to turn around and come back. I've learned how to make the most of these waiting periods.

If I'm waiting for a kid to finish practice, I have a list of things to do rather than sit there bored. I keep a packet of Windex wipes in the car so I can quickly clean the console and windows. I always have a book to read—if not a physical book, a digital book on my phone. If my child has to arrive to a game an hour early, I bring my laptop or printed manuscript to work on in the car until game time. Social media is part of my job, so I might catch up on reading blogs or posting to Facebook. I also look forward to catching up on personal calls at this time. I've even brought greeting cards and filled them out while waiting.

If you don't get much time to yourself, this waiting time can be a dream come true. Borrow an audio book from the library. Read a magazine. Buy the decadent latte and sip it in the privacy of your mini-van.

Parents shuttling to and from practice with younger kids will not be able to savor these moments, unfortunately, but you can pack things for the little ones to do. If the weather is nice, try to find a park close by for them to run around and play. If it's raining, keep sticker books or washable markers and paper in the car. Pop a cartoon into the DVD player or crank up a sing-a-long CD.

Maybe the driving/waiting comes at the witching hour. Your younger kids are tired, hungry, and fighting. Your patience wears thin. I know. It's not fun. Instead of accepting the shouting and fighting, do your best to make the time pass pleasantly. Buy coloring books, markers, stickers, cards, travel games, outside toys like a Frisbee or small ball and store them in a bin in the trunk. This will help the kids channel their energy. And buy that decadent coffee drink no matter what. Make it a large.

Stock your vehicle at the beginning of the sport's season. If games are outdoors, throw a few camping chairs in the trunk and leave them there until the season ends. Ditto for an umbrella and an old blanket. You might want to pack a box of non-perishable snacks and some bottles of water just in case practice runs over and everyone is starving.

Uniform Care

Parents, if you're staring at a pile of football, lacrosse, baseball, soccer, or other stained uniforms, I feel your pain.

Some uniforms are easy to clean. Frankly, washing my daughter's cross country uniform was simple. Toss it into the washing machine by itself and let it air dry. Done! My son's baseball uniforms on the other hand...the worst. Grass stains, red clay, mud splashes—you name it— they cling to the uniform like hungry ticks on a dog. And I'm not washing filthy uniforms once a week, oh no, I might be washing them every other day.

My uniform strategy is to aggressively fight stains. I rely on several things to do this: pre-treatment spray, detergent bars, and a soaking formula. Check the label of the uniform for care instructions. Hot water or cold water, gentle wash versus regular wash, and drying methods need to be followed.

All of the uniforms I've dealt with can be machine washed. I always treat stains first. Either spray pre-treatment liquid on all the big stains, or wet the area and rub a detergent bar over the spots. Then fill a washtub or large pail with hot water and a scoop of laundry detergent. Soak the uniform pieces for a few hours or overnight. Drain the water and rub the stained material together to try to scrub out the marks as much as possible. They don't have to be completely gone at this point. Launder the pieces as usual. If the stains persist, repeat the pretreatment and soaking, then launder again.

Bleach doesn't always work. If you have white uniforms, go ahead and try it, but treating and scrubbing are your best bets.

I rarely put any uniform piece in the dryer. Most need to air dry.

Wash uniforms as soon as possible after games and practices for the best results. The longer a stain sits, the more it sets.

Fundraising

The final practical matter is fundraising. Sends shivers down your spine, doesn't it? I know. Most parents don't like fundraising—I personally dread it—but it's a necessary part of sports. If your child is on a competitive team, you'll probably have to raise money. Fundraising must be a team effort with every family responsible.

I'm only going to touch on this topic because it could fill an entire book on its own. I realize some of the methods listed below could be considered gambling, so please do not feel you need to cross a personal ethical line to raise money for your team. There are plenty of other ways to raise money, or a cash donation might be the way to go.

One of my most popular blog articles is "Fundraising Methods for Youth Sports,"[14] also titled, "How We Raised Five Figures to Send Our 12U Baseball Team on a Weeklong Tournament in Cooperstown, NY." I'm listing the highlights here. Please check with your local and state laws before implementing any fundraising strategies.

- Sell products (pizza kits, wrapping paper, chocolates, laundry detergent) that allow your organization to keep a percentage of the profits.
- Hold a 50/50 raffle. This means selling raffle tickets, and one winner will be selected on a predetermined date to win 50% of the money raised. Your team keeps the other 50%. For this to work, set a mandatory amount of tickets each family on the team must sell. Decide on a reasonable price per ticket. Set a time limit. Give the team at least two weeks to sell them before the winner is drawn. Parents usually sell them to friends, family, and coworkers. Talk to local organizers of other sports and ask if the players on your

team can sell the tickets at one of their concessions. Have the team dress in uniform for
this. Make sure you collect names and phone
numbers on the tickets to contact the winner. The winning ticket should be drawn by
someone who is not involved with your
team. If you opt to do a 50/50 raffle, organization is important. Have one team parent in
charge of collecting all the tickets and money from the other parents. You could give
each family a spreadsheet with spots for the
name, ticket number(s), phone number, and
amount paid. Make packets for each kid with
a large clear plastic bag, the tickets they're
supposed to sell, and the spreadsheet. Encourage them to keep the tickets and the
money they collect in the plastic bag. Have
them turn in the bag containing money,
tickets sold, and any leftover tickets on a
certain date.

- Corporate sponsors. Encourage everyone on
  the team to ask for corporate sponsors. We
  type up a form to hand out with different
  levels of sponsorship listed. Businesses can
  donate $250, $500, or $1000. It's good to list
  a reason why you're asking for money.
  "We're raising money to send *list your team*
  to the State Tournament, and we need your
  help." Put a contact number on the form and
  clearly state who the check should be made
  out to and the address to mail it. If your
  team is part of a nonprofit organization, remind the donors this is a tax write-off.
  There are a lot of rules for collecting money
  for nonprofits, so be sure to study and fol-

low them. Go to my website, jillkemer-
er.com/books/game-on/, for a down-
loadable pdf sample letter. You won't be
able to modify it, but it will give you an idea
of how to create your own letter.

- Reverse Raffle. If you need to raise a huge
chunk of money (five figures), consider
hosting a reverse raffle night. For a good
overview of how reverse raffles work, check
out "Fundraising Idea: How to Run a Reverse Raffle Fundraiser," on Fundrais-
ingIP.com.[15] The price of the ticket depends
on your overall costs. If you're including
dinner and beverages, the price of one ticket
could be anywhere from $20 to $80. Keep in
mind it's harder to sell tickets at higher pric-
es. You will need a lot of volunteers, one or
two people to head up the event, and trustworthy people to collect money. Some of
the things to line up: rental space, catering,
insurance, and a DJ to run the reverse raffle.
You could host pay-to-play games at the
event, also. I highly recommend hosting a silent auction during the reverse raffle. One or
two parents will need to coordinate the silent auction items. To ensure you have
enough items to sell, make it mandatory
each family on the team provides one gift
basket to raffle off. Then have parents ask
local businesses to donate coupons, gift cer-
tificates, or actual products. All silent auction proceeds go to your team. Consider
investing in a credit card reader for a phone
so that people can pay with credit or debit
cards. These readers are inexpensive, and

most providers charge a small percentage of the sale.

- Car washes/bake sales. A good car wash can raise a couple hundred dollars in one afternoon. Bake sales in the right place (a local festival or similar venue) can be lucrative, too.
- Sporting event squares. You basically create a ten-by-ten grid on a piece of paper. There will be exactly 100 squares, Number the top and sides from zero to nine. You then sell squares for a set dollar amount for the specific game. The Superbowl, a college rivalry football game, or any big game works well. Check the score at the end of the first quarter, half-time, and the third quarter. The name in the square with those numbers wins a small amount of money. The name in the square of the final score wins a larger amount, maybe 25% of the total. The rest of the money goes to your team. One person needs to be in charge of making the square sheet and collecting money. The rest of the team sells squares. It's important to not oversell or undersell these squares as the number of them is always one hundred.
- Concessions. Do you sell concessions at your games? Is there another local venue where you could sell concessions for a portion of the profit? Try local colleges, ice arenas, minor league baseball stadiums, even amusement parks.
- Cleaning the stands. Local sports arenas often pay teams to come in and sweep their

bleachers. Your team could do this for a fundraising boost.

- Hold a Harvest Party/Family Night and charge a small admission fee. Paint pumpkins and raffle them off. Sell inexpensive balloons, kiddy items, hot dogs, beverages. Host free game stations with parents running them. A corn hole toss, face painting, ring toss, and bounce house are fun for young kids.

- Set up an account (GoFundMe, FlipGive) for anyone to donate. Maybe Grandma and Grandpa will kick in twenty dollars. Or your siblings/friends who live out of state. You never know who might contribute.

- Many restaurants will host a fundraising day for a local team. Your team will take home a portion of the profits of food purchases during a set time. Invite everyone you know— we all have to eat anyhow, right?

There are hundreds of ways to raise money for your team if you're willing and organized. As I mentioned earlier, before you begin fundraising be sure to familiarize yourself with the laws. If your team is affiliated with a nonprofit organization, you need to follow the rules closely. Keep meticulous financial records, and always have more than one person in charge of the overall funds. The last thing you want is all your time and effort wasted through mismanagement.

Truths to Take Away:

1. Being prepared will make your life easier.

2. If finances are tight, do what's best for your family.

3. Pack your car with items you'll need during the season, whether it's camping chairs, a blanket, umbrella, activities for siblings, bleacher cushions, or other items.

4. Feeding our families during busy seasons can be challenging. List quick and easy meals, bake a double batch of a casserole and freeze half, use a slow cooker, and plan ahead.

5. Use the waiting periods to catch up on work or calls, or simply enjoy some private time.

6. Treat and wash uniforms as soon as possible after games and practices to prevent permanent stains.

7. Fundraising needs to be a group effort.

Acknowledgements

When I decided to write this book, I had no idea how much my attitude would change. For years I'd been merely surviving sports, not understanding how the highs and lows shaped our kids. By the time I finished writing it, I had a game plan in place to keep sports in perspective and to truly enjoy watching my kids play.

I'm thankful to the Lord for helping me see my flaws and putting it on my heart to share this with other parents who are struggling through their kids' sports. By God's grace I have the tools I need to fight the insecurity, pride, and competitiveness sports bring out of me. I fail sometimes, but it's okay. I'm not perfect and never will be.

I'm also grateful for all of the information published about youth sports in America. The articles and statistics I read opened my eyes to the false beliefs parents cling to about sports.

Thank you to my husband, Scott, who encouraged me to write this book from the minute I said, "I have this idea..." Thank you for your patience with our kids, for being a true role model to them, for believing in me, for being an early reader, and for all the alternate titles. I love you.

Thank you to Wendy Paine Miller for not only listening to my sports complaints ages before I ever thought of writing this book, but who also caught my vision, critiqued the content, and lifted my spirits over and over again. Oh, and let's not forget my title meltdown! Thank you!

Thanks to writer friends who encouraged me so many times—Jessica Patch, Sarah Forgrave, Janice Boekhoff, Susan Tuttle, Patrice Kavanaugh, Julie Jarnagin, Jill Buteyn, Mindy Obenhaus, Becky Wade, and Dani Pettrey. What would I do without you?

Thanks to my local writer friends—the entire Maumee Valley Romance Authors, Inc. crew—with special thanks to Constance Phillips and Sloan Parker for your technical advice and patience answering my many questions. I owe you both coffees!

Thank you to my agent, Rachel Kent, for your wisdom, insight, and help with my career. I am so thankful to partner with you.

Finally, thank YOU, dear readers. If some part of this book helps you in any way, please leave a review and share it with your friends. I pray this book blesses you and your children.

Notes

1. Character. Dictionary.com. Dictionary.com Unabridged. Random House, Inc.
    http://www.dictionary.com/browse/character
    (accessed: October 26, 2016) Character. Merriam-Webster.com. Merriam-Webster. Merriam-Webster, Inc. http://www.merriam-webster.com/dictionary/character (accessed: October 26, 2016)

2. "Organization Profile | US Youth Soccer." US Youth Soccer.
    http://www.usyouthsoccer.org/media_kit/organizationprofile/ (accessed October 27, 2016)

3. "Key Statistics | US Youth Soccer." US Youth Soccer.
    http://www.usyouthsoccer.org/media_kit/keystatistics/ (accessed October 27, 2016)

4. "Odds of a High School Athlete Playing College Sports." ScholarshipStats.com.
    http://www.scholarshipstats.com/varsityodds.html Statistics are compiled and edited by Patrick O'Rourke, CPA, Washington, DC (accessed October 27, 2016)

5. "Chances of a High School Athlete Getting an Athletic Scholarship." ScholarshipStat.com. http://www.scholarshipstats.com/scholarshipodds.html Statistics are compiled and edited by Patrick O'Rourke, CPA, Washington, DC (accessed October 27, 2016)

6. Barr, Cecillia. "College Athletic Scholarships: NCAA & NAIA Sports Scholarships." Debt.org News. https://www.debt.org/students/athletic-scholarships/ (accessed October 27, 2016)

7. Frank, David. "Make Sure You Meet the NCAA and NAIA College Academic Requirement." AhtleticScholarships.net. http://www.athleticscholarships.net/academic-requirements.htm (accessed November 19, 2016)

8. Ann Kearns Davoren and Seunghyun Hwang. "Mind, Body and Sport: Depression and Anxiety Prevalence in Student-athletes." NCAA.org. 2014. http://www.ncaa.org/health-and-safety/sport-science-institute/mind-body-and-sport-depression-and-anxiety-prevalence-student-athletes (accessed October 27, 2016)

9. "The Warm Milk Journal." The Warm Milk Journal. http://www.thewarmmilkjournal.com/ (accessed November 29, 2016)

10. Staff, Mayo Clinic. "Performance Enhancing Drugs and Teen Athletes." MayoClinic.org. March 11, 2015. http://www.mayoclinic.org/healthy-lifestyle/tween-and-teen-health/in-depth/performance-enhancing-drugs/art-20046620 (accessed November 19, 2016)

11. "Athletes and Eating Disorders." NationalEatingDisorders.org. https://www.nationaleatingdisorders.org/athletes-and-eating-disorders (accessed November 19, 2016)

12. *NEDA TOOLKIT for Coaches & Trainers.* NationalEatingDisorders.org. http://www.nationaleatingdisorders.org/sites/default/files/Toolkits/CoachandTrainerToolkit.pdf (accessed November 19, 2016)

13. "AMSSM - American Medical Society for Sports Medicine." AMSSM - American Medical Society for Sports Medicine. http://www.amssm.org/Publications.html (accessed October 28, 2016)

14. Jill Kemerer. "Fundraising Methods for Youth Sports Teams." Jill Kemerer. January 24, 2014. http://jillkemerer.blogspot.com/2014/01/fundraising-methods-for-youth-sports.html (accessed November 02, 2016).

15. @fundraisingip. "Fundraising Idea: How to Run a Reverse Raffle Fundraiser." Fundraising Letters, Checklists, How Tos and Event Ideas. 2015. http://www.fundraisingip.com/fundraising/reverse-raffle-fundraiser/ (accessed December 07, 2016)

ABOUT THE AUTHOR

Jill Kemerer is a wife, mother of two, and a full-time writer. In addition to her Christian romance novels published through Harlequin™ Love Inspired, her work has appeared in Guideposts: The Best Angel Stories 2015, Chicken Soup for the Soul: It's Christmas! as well as the short story and recipe collection, *A Recipe for Romance*. Before pursuing a career in writing, she graduated magna cum laude with a bachelor's degree in electrical engineering.

Jill's favorite hobby is reading, and she always has a stack of books and magazines on hand. She loves spoiling her mini-dachshund, eating M&Ms, drinking coffee, gushing over fluffy animals, and taking long nature walks. She resides in Ohio. Jill loves connecting with readers, so please visit her website, jillkemerer.com, email her at jill@jillkemerer.com, and sign up for her newsletter to stay in the loop about her novels and giveaways.

CONNECT WITH JILL

Follow Jill Kemerer:

Facebook:
http://www.facebook.com/AuthorJillKemerer
Twitter:
http://twitter.com/jillkemerer
Instagram:
http://instagram.com/jillkemerer/
Pinterest:
http://pinterest.com/jillkemerer/
Goodreads:
http://www.goodreads.com/jillkemerer
Amazon Author Page
http://amazon.com/author/jillkemerer

If you enjoyed this book, consider leaving a review on Amazon, Goodreads, or other retailers. Reviews help readers find my books! Thank you!

Made in the USA
Lexington, KY
24 March 2017